#HOPE DEALERS

THE CHANGES, CHALLENGES AND CALLINGS OF SAYING YES!

LANCE LANG

Published by:

ISBN: 978-1974405473
Printed in the United States of America
Library of Congress Cataloging-in-Publication Data

All scripture quotations, unless otherwise indicated are taken from The Holy Bible, English Standard Version® (ESV®) Copyright © 2001 by Crossway, a publishing ministry of Good News Publishers. All rights reserved. ESV Text Edition: 2007.

For information regarding author interviews or speaking engagements, please contact the public relations department – Lance@LanceLang.com.

A WORD BEFORE

THIS WON'T BE EASY

It's human nature to love things that are easy; losing hope is easy.

I know that seems like a downer start to a book about hope, but I want to make sure we're clear about what's at stake. Because there's a huge difference between the reality of this world and what we're told about it. Negativity sells and so that's what we're bombarded with. We're constantly told that things are getting worse and worse, that the end is nigh, that barbarians are at the gate, that life is too hard and that our difficulties are too strong. We hear it so much that we begin to think that negative vision of the world is the only one. The "real" one. The authentic one.

We also can't forget about another view of the world: that of the false positive. This is the view filled with inauthentic social media feeds, the plastered smiles, the everything-is-fine-here phoniness that all too often plagues us. We dare not admit that our lives are a mess—what will everyone think of us?! And so we pretend and we post scriptures about walking in victory so that no one knows we can't even get off the floor.

In my experience, most people have become so numb to these alternate realities. We just accept that what we experience is the way it has to be, and we stay in our deserts and we occasionally swallow our own saliva and we call that a thirst-quencher.

But that's a lie. It's all a lie. We've forgotten the refreshing stream that is authentic, genuine living. I look at the world and I see that it's full of people who are radically changing their lives for the better. Minute by minute, hour by hour. Miracles have been transported off the Sunday School craft table and into the world I see. Hopeless marriages are being restored. Addicted people are being set free. Children are being reunited with parents. Desperate mothers and fathers of addicts are looking through their pain and finding hope and purpose in their lives.

I wrote this book hoping that it can be the lens you place in front of your eyes so you could see the world for the beautiful, hope-filled thing that it really, truly is.

I wrote this book to extend hope to those who have lost it. Like a big box of fresh French fries, hope is meant to be shared. I also wrote this book as a monument to those seeking freedom. Like the monument of stones that Joshua had brought from the bed of the Jordan River (it's a great story; read it in Joshua 3:7-4:24), hope is a concrete reminder of where God has brought us from—and where He is taking us.

I wrote this book to be a glass of water in your desert. But not just to give you a refreshing taste of hope but also to show you where the stream is located so you can build a home there.

So you can start bottling that water in your story and sharing it with those around you. Maybe you'll get to take them to the stream. Maybe they'll build a house next door.

The truth is we all have a HopeDealer story. The qualifications are simple:

- Be a human
- Have a story
- Be willing to tell it

That's it! The stories you will read in this book are of normal everyday people. Flawed, broken, hurting, addicted men and women just like you. The only difference between where they are and where you may be today is that they've said YES to telling the world what happened. And that simple three letter word can be the hardest word to say. But the freedom on the other side of that YES is life-changing!

So, dear reader, this book is for you. It's not about me and is not even really about the people you'll read about. It's here to show you that hope is real, that people really do change, and that God is at work in this wonder-filled, beauty-filled world we all share. My hope is that by the time you close this book, you'll be inspired enough to know that you can make a difference and start dealing hope.

Hope is never easy. But then again, nothing worth having ever is.

#ONE

DEFINING A HOPEDEALER

You're going to read the word *HopeDealer* a lot in this book, so let's make sure we all know what I mean when I use it. It's a promise that I claimed for myself when I first started getting sober. I was not only a drug user in my past, I was also a drug dealer, and I wanted to reclaim that idea, so I started calling myself a HopeDealer. I even started signing all my social media posts with the hashtag "#HopeDealer" and it stuck.

But I'm not the only HopeDealer in the world, nor do I want to be! I want everyone to become one! But what is a HopeDealer? There are so many facets and ways to describe a HopeDealer:

A HopeDealer is someone who has gone through pain and now has a purpose.

A HopeDealer is a survivor who is willing to tell their story.

A HopeDealer is someone who has found hope and who is willing to tell others about it.

A HopeDealer is a spreader of love, grace, and forgiveness.

A HopeDealer is someone who has traded pain for purpose,

sorrow for sobriety, and failures for freedom.

A HopeDealer is a flawed person bragging on a flawless God.

These all get at the truth, but the more I've thought about it, the more I realize: **a HopeDealer is really just anyone who is willing to say YES.**

YES to sharing their pain.

YES to finding the hope.

YES to owning their past.

YES to acknowledging their present.

YES to embracing their future.

In other words, *anyone* can be a HopeDealer.

Your story is yours. No one else has lived the story that you've lived. Everything that's ever happened to you has culminated in the unique being that is you. At the same time, you share so many of the broad strokes of your story with others.

Novelists and screenwriters know about basic story structure. Almost all the stories that we love share a similar structure. There's an impetuous hero, a wise mentor who provides key guidance, a quest, a failure along that quest that provides a learning opportunity, and then a final resolution where our hero either completes their quest successfully (a happy ending) or unsuccessfully (the opposite ending).

Storytellers have spun this structure into countless individual stories that all become unique through the details. From *Star Wars* to *Alice in Wonderland* to *Beauty and the Beast* to every possible spin on Spider-Man, artists have used an underlying structure to find commonality while changing the specifics to make their story deliciously their own.

Our own stories are the same, and I know this because I've seen it over and over. I talk to men and women all the time who have made a mess of their lives and the story beats are depressingly familiar—but each of those stories is also unique to that person and has had a devastating effect on them as an individual, radiating out from them to inflict further damage on their loved ones.

In other words, while the struggles of life are as diverse as the population, many of us share common plights. You can say YES to your unique story and find common ground with others. When you tell your story, others can hear their own story contained within, which unlocks what I call the power of shared pain.

What does this mean in practice? It means you can be a HopeDealer.

If you've overcome the pain of a divorce, you can be a HopeDealer.

If you've worked through grief over losing someone you loved, you can be a HopeDealer.

If you're managing your depression or anxiety, you can be a

HopeDealer.

If you've successfully walked through an addiction to pornography, you can be a HopeDealer.

If you've kicked heroin, you can be a HopeDealer.

If you've shredded tons of weight, you can be a HopeDealer.

If you've beat cancer, you can be a HopeDealer.

If you've overcome an eating disorder, you can be a HopeDealer.

There is really no limit to who can be HopeDealer, because we all have some HOPE to give!

That's what a HopeDealer is. But what does a HopeDealer do? We will talk more and more about this throughout the book. But what I am challenging you to consider is this:

A HopeDealer is one willing to share their pain and their past with anyone who needs what they have! That means a HopeDealer looks at the dark cave that is their story and, rather than be afraid of or intimidated by it, steps into it. And they take a pickax with them because they know they're going to find plenty of precious stones to mine, bits of gold or diamonds that the pressure and hardship of their lives have created. HopeDealers bring those riches up to the surface so they can share it and enrich the lives of those around them. HopeDealers turn their hurt into hope and they never hoard it.

A HopeDealer can be anyone, anytime, anyplace. If God has

given you a HopeDealer story, I'm going to encourage you to say YES to that story and to start telling it. And I want to show you how.

The HopeDealer Verse

I do a lot of speaking in churches. It's one of the many privileges of doing what I do. In fact, almost every Sunday I find myself in a different church, ready to take the stage and share from God's hopeful heart. And over the years I've been doing that, just before I've gone up, I've recited this verse to myself:

"I waited patiently for the Lord to help me, and he turned to me and heard my cry. He lifted me out of the pit of despair, out of the mud and the mire. He set my feet on solid ground and steadied me as I walked along. He has given me a new song to sing, a hymn of praise to our God. Many will see what he has done and be amazed. They will put their trust in the Lord." (Psalm 40:1-3, NLT)

This is the HopeDealer verse. All of us can relate to this, can't we? God has rescued us in some form or fashion (and the longer I live, the more I realize He *keeps* rescuing me) and sets us up on solid ground. He restores us. He steadies us. He puts us back on the road we were meant to be on until we got sidetracked and fell into that dumb pit in the first place.

And then He puts that new song in our mouths.

The HopeDealer decides that song is not something they

hum to themselves while they're driving to work or while they're loading the dishwasher. No, the HopeDealer has decided that song is the soundtrack of their life and is something to be sung *to an audience*. HopeDealers sing that song so that others can hear it, recognize the melody as something familiar, and dig deeper into the lyrics to discover a hope they didn't know they could have.

This verse shows us the promise of a life devoted to helping others find peace and a chance through the pain of our past. When we sing about our time in the pit—and how God lifted us out— we're singing our specific comeback story. And my favorite part of that verse (oh, who am I kidding; I love the whole thing) is the product that comes when we are willing to sing our song: that *many* will see what *He* has done and be amazed...

What's crazy about God and the Bible is how you can stumble across a verse or two and how they feel as though they have been specifically written for *you!* That's what this verse feels like to me. This verse is my life, spelled out in 82 words. But now I'm going to take a few extra words to tell you more.

The HopeDealer verse starts with "I waited patiently for the Lord," but I also like to think of it as the Lord waiting patiently on *me*. Because from high school to professional life, from a little pot here and there to a carefully managed cocktail of prescription drug abuse, it took me forever (about a decade, actually) to decide I'd hit rock bottom.

But then, "He heard my cry." I was on the job, working for

my Uncle Pat, and unsuccessfully hiding an all-consuming drug habit. I was crying out without even realizing it, and the Lord heard my cry. He came into my pit of despair in the form of my Uncle Pat. He got in my face and challenged me and that's when I knew it was time to give up and let God pull me out of that thing. (There's a whole lot more to the story, by the way. I tell it more completely in my first book, *Hope Is Alive*.)

"He lifted me out." I went to treatment and everything began to change for me. I began to learn how to surrender so my life could be restored. God used treatment to put me back on solid ground.

And then, the greatest honor of all, "He gave me a new song to sing." A song called Hope Is Alive. And that song is far more beautiful than anything I could've ever imagined while I was in that pit or even when my feet were back on solid ground. Now, God is using this song to radically change the lives of drug addicts, alcoholics, and those who love them. Our primary focus is our Mentoring Homes, where over 70 men and women currently live. It's in these homes where God is raising up a crop of HopeDealers.

This book is filled with incredible stories of the HopeDealers that Hope is Alive has had the privilege of working with, impacting, or being somehow part of their story. It's full of people who said YES.

Part of being a HopeDealer is understanding that God is going to put opportunities to say YES in front of you, and it's up to you to keep your eyes open for those opportunities so you can seize them.

My hope story took forever to get started because I kept running from my YES. I instead chose to go through a bunch of pain as I turned away from my calling over and over, until I finally said YES to my Uncle Pat when he told me I needed to get help. Then I said YES to treatment. And the YESes just continued from there.

While I was just a week into treatment, they found out I was a pastor's kid and so they asked me to lead a Bible study. I felt totally unqualified. I thought, "This is the stuff I've always run from doing. I've only been here a week and they're labeling me as the Bible study guy right out of the gate?" I didn't realize at the time that this was God already putting an opportunity in front of me.

I was a mess, but I still decided to say YES. Indeed, sometimes it's best to say YES inside a mess! Maybe you're wading through a whole pool of awful circumstances or maybe you're getting buried under the consequences of your bad decisions. Are you at least moving in the right direction, even if you're only taking one slow step at a time? Then you can still say YES! That was me, barely into treatment and still saying YES to this Bible study. I knew I was heading in the right direction, I was surrounded by the right people, I had wise mentors speaking into my life, and the Holy Spirit was prompting me to do it.

From the outside, it looked like the beginnings of a bad idea, but there inside my mess, I somehow knew it would be exactly what I needed. Besides, I was tired of saying NO to God. I'd been doing that for ten years! I'm so glad I said YES to this opportunity.

I started leading that Bible study and it literally started with me and one other guy. 10:15 in the cafeteria every morning, just the two of us. But I kept saying YES and, before you know it, there was another guy. And then another. And then two more. We had a good group going by the time I left.

And then I got to say YES to telling my story for the first time at a church. Today, I've shared my story over 700 times in 300 different churches! And the YESes continue… I got to say YES to writing a book. Which led to another and then yet another. Then I got to say YES to opening a house.

YES. YES. YES.

This book is a story of YESes.

I hope you'll add your YES by the end of it.

#TWO

SAYING YES CHANGES EVERYTHING

I don't think there is any greater honor than being a HopeDealer. To think that the God of the universe walked with me through my craziest of days and still loved me enough to make good out of it—it still blows my mind!

But what's even crazier is that He has given me a passionate desire to tell you that He is doing the same thing in your life as well. I always think of the story of Joseph in Genesis, where his jealous brothers sell him into slavery in Egypt and God puts him in a place not only to rescue his own family from starvation but also to save the entire nation. When all the dust has settled, Joseph tells his brothers, "You intended to harm me, but God intended it all for good. He brought me to this position so I could save the lives of many people." (Genesis 50:20, NLT)

My thing is, I sold *myself* into slavery in Egypt through my drug use, and I caused myself a lot of pain, but God has turned that pain around and used it for His glory so that a lot of people can be saved. He's always working things together for our good, and there's no curve ball we can throw that God can't hit out of the park.

A lot of my pain was self-inflicted, but sometimes other people hurt us. We say YES to God and they tell us NO. What then? As it just so happens, I know how you feel.

When I was about 6 months clean, I was offered a job at a treatment center and I jumped on it. It felt so great to be connecting with a bunch of people who were going through the part of the journey I'd just completed, to lend them an empathetic ear. I could encourage them in what they were going through because I'd just gone through it myself. I was ready to take up this mantle as both a ministry and a lifelong career. I began to envision myself in this role for years, thinking about what it might be like five, ten, twenty years down the road.

And then, nine months later, I got fired.

I was devastated. All my plans had just crumbled to dust in front of me. Me! A recent drug addict still learning how to live a sober life! Things could've gotten really, really bad. I was deeply hurt, publicly humiliated, and completely confused. What was I going to do with my life now?

I retreated to the back patio of my parents' house to lick my wounds and talk things over with my dad, and over the course of those conversations, I began to dream about what would become Hope Is Alive.

Six months after I was fired, that dream was a full-fledged reality. God made so much good out of that horribly painful situation. God honored my YES and redeemed my former employer's NO. God breathed into me an entirely new vision for my life, a vision that far exceeded anything I'd ever imagined while I was working at that treatment center. He was preparing to use my pain for His purpose, and I had no idea what would happen next.

Maybe this has happened to you. Maybe you thought you were on the right track, saying YES to God, when someone suddenly stood in front of you with a great big NO. You've been hurt by those you thought were going to help. You've been preparing to fly only to discover backbiters have been plucking out your wings, feather by feather.

Your responsibility, same as mine, was not to try to take charge and make results happen on God's behalf. Your responsibility, same as mine, was to say YES and trust God for the rest. That's what I had to learn, and it's what I did, and God, as is His way, proved Himself *extremely* trustworthy.

Hope HQ

Here's the way the rest of this book is going to go: I'm going to be a HopeDealer, and occasionally I'm going to turn the floor over to some other HopeDealers I know. Now, my world is the world of addiction, and most of these HopeDealers I've met as a result of Hope Is Alive. So I'm going to be mining my story of saying YES—which is largely the story of Hope Is Alive—and I'm going to be sharing the stories of some other HopeDealers I've encountered as I've lived out the story of HIA.

These are the stories I know. It's my hope that, by the end of this book, you'll be inspired by these stories and start thinking about all the stories *you* know and how *those* might inspire someone else to tell the stories *they* know. It's really amazing what God can do when we say YES, how He can use us. How He can put a huge vision into a measly little drug addict who had hope in his heart and YES in his mouth.

The first part of the vision was to get a house. I wanted a place where men could come, live, and change their lives forever. I wanted them to have a home full of hope, where they could catch a vision for a sober life, to learn what I was learning: that living sober is *way* more fun than anything else.

At first I wanted to buy the house, but I knew I couldn't afford it, so I started looking at other ways to get a home. I was still heavily involved in Alcoholics Anonymous, and I mentioned this dream to my sponsor, who told me about a home he knew about that was available for lease-purchase. He gave me the contact information and Allyson and I went to check it out.

As soon as we walked in, we felt immediately like this could be the one. The more we walked through it, the more we *knew* it was the one. We began to fall in love with it, but we knew we had to be up front with the owner about why we wanted it. Not everyone would be as enthusiastic as we were about filling a house with former drug addicts learning how to live sober, but we were hoping he'd at least be receptive to the idea.

So I went to the owner, a man by the name of Kyle Allen, and told him that I wanted it and what I wanted it for. I was trying to be clever and tiptoe around the "sobriety" and "recovery" parts of our mission, telling him that I wanted to open a place where men could have a fresh start to get back on their feet and that sort of thing, when Kyle cut me off.

"Lance," he said, "I was going to turn that into a sober living house if you didn't want it. So if that's how you want to use it, then it's all yours."

The very first person I went to said YES! This was amazing confirmation for Hope Is Alive in our early goings, and very much something we needed. We had our Hope Headquarters.

The First Two HopeDealers

So we had a house; now we needed some people (other than me!) to live in it. I moved in and began to actively recruit some other guys to join me in this great mission. The first was a man who'd been in treatment while I was working at the treatment center, and he was totally on board. We set a move-in date and he was ready to go.

But the day before he came in, I got word of another guy who needed a landing spot pronto. He'd been working for a treatment center and his job had just ended; he had nowhere to go and wanted to maintain his sobriety. Hope HQ was the perfect spot for him.

So in one day we went from zero residents to two, and Matt

and Jeff became the first two members of our original five.

In a way, this reminds me of the story of Gideon. You may remember him. We read about Gideon in the book of Judges, where we learn that the Israelites have been under the thumb of an oppressive power for several years. God decides that the time has come to deliver them and so He calls Gideon to the task.

Where does God find Gideon? Minding his own business, threshing wheat in secret. Nevertheless, God calls Gideon to deliver his people, and Gideon says YES.

Now, Gideon's wasn't a full-throated, fire-in-the-belly YES. Gideon's was a hesitant, are-you-really-sure YES. But it was still a YES! Gideon just wanted to make sure that God was actually calling *him* to this monumental task. Gideon was just a dude of no consequence from a small family that was also of no consequence—he felt he needed assurance that he was actually hearing God correctly, so he kind of whispered his YES. At first.

After seeing some signs (Gideon's story is where we get the phrase, "Put out a fleece;" it's from Judges 6:36-40) and feeling more confident, Gideon's whispered YES turns into a spoken YES. He's learning that he can trust God, and that if he just follows what God tells him to do, he can believe God will bless his obedience.

And then this is where it gets crazy. I don't know much about the military or about battles, but I do have this much figured out: if you want to win a war, it helps to have a lot of soldiers. But that's not always the case with God!

Gideon used his YES to raise up an army of over 30,000 soldiers, but God wanted to do things differently. In fact, God even says as much: "You have too many warriors with you. If I let all of you fight the Midianites, the Israelites will boast to me that they saved themselves by their own strength." (Judges 7:2, NLT) So God tells Gideon to send home the people who are too timid or afraid, the ones who aren't ready to give a full YES to the effort, and more than two-thirds of the army heads home.

But that was still too many, so God whittled it down to just 300 soldiers, and you know what Gideon said in the face of those odds? He still said YES! He obeyed, because he trusted that God was going to do something miraculous.

And boy, He did. See, this is one of the many things I love about God: we always have our way of thinking about things, our standard ways of doing things, and God says, "You know what? I love your heart, but there's a better way."

You probably know this part. God tells Gideon what to do: use fire and noise and the bad guys will take care of themselves, and though it may have sounded crazy at first, Gideon still said YES.

And it worked.

To recap: God found this humble guy, called him to great things, and the guy just kept saying YES along the way. YES to the call. YES to raising an army. YES to decreasing that army by two-thirds. YES again to decreasing that army all the way down to 300. YES to this crazy-sounding plan with rams' horns and clay pots of fire.

I love the way God works. He just leads us along the way, putting a bunch of YESes in front of us so that when we look back, we can say, "Holy mackerel, this sure would've seemed nuts if I'd known where I was heading, but I'm so glad I said YES to each of these steps."

The HopeDealer rarely sees the full picture. God may give you a vision for something big, but He rarely gives you a step-by-step instruction manual so that you know how you're going to get there. No, more often than not, God does things for HopeDealers like He did for Gideon. He just shows the next step and trusts you to say YES. And then you get to say YES to the second step. Then to the third.

That's also the story of HIA. I knew I just needed to keep saying YES, but I had no idea the numbers of people who would be impacted by those continued YESes. I've heard so many HopeDealer stories come out of the step-by-step YESes that we've been saying here at Hope Is Alive. These are the stories that I want to share with you over the rest of this book. Gideon-style stories of HopeDealers who have tired of saying NO and who've decided just to keep saying YES.

It's time to start meeting some HopeDealers. It's time to find your YES.

#THREE

STARTED FROM THE BOTTOM

"You're blessed when you're at the end of your rope. With less of you there is more of God and his rule." (Matthew 5:3, MSG)

I love the Beatitudes so much. If you aren't familiar with that terminology, the Beatitudes are the first few verses of Jesus' famous Sermon on the Mount, the linchpin of all His teachings. The complete sermon takes up two whole chapters in Matthew, but I want to focus on chapter 5, verses 3-12 for the remainder of this book. And because I really love the modern language of it, we're going to look at the Message translation of this passage, an important one that really sets the table for the rest of Jesus' teaching. Let's read the whole thing:

"You're blessed when you're at the end of your rope. With less of you there is more of God and his rule.

"You're blessed when you feel you've lost what is most dear to you. Only then can you be embraced by the One most dear to you.

"You're blessed when you're content with just who you are—no more, no less. That's the moment you find yourselves proud owners of everything that can't be bought.

"You're blessed when you've worked up a good appetite for God. He's food and drink in the best meal you'll ever eat.

"You're blessed when you care. At the moment of being 'care-full,' you find yourselves cared for.

"You're blessed when you get your inside world—your mind and heart—put right. Then you can see God in the outside world.

"You're blessed when you can show people how to cooperate instead of compete or fight. That's when you discover who you really are, and your place in God's family.

"You're blessed when your commitment to God provokes persecution. The persecution drives you even deeper into God's kingdom.

"Not only that—count yourselves blessed every time people put you down or throw you out or speak lies about you to discredit me. What it means is that the truth is too close for comfort and they are uncomfortable. You can be glad when that happens—give a cheer, even!—for though they don't like it, I do! And all heaven applauds. And know that you are in good company. My prophets and witnesses have always gotten into this kind of trouble." (Matthew 5:3-12, MSG)

I don't know about you, but that gets me fired up! I mean, I'm not crazy about the "persecution" stuff at the end, but the rest of it is so counter-intuitively inspiring. And I also love it because I think the Beatitudes mirror the journey of Hope Is Alive so well. If Psalm 40:1-3 is the HopeDealer verse, then the Beatitudes are the HIA verses.

Because of this parallel, we're going to use the Beatitudes for the rest of this book as a way to examine the remaining history of Hope Is Alive and the HopeDealers we've been so blessed to get to know along the way.

For example, the first verse says you're blessed when you're at the end of your rope. This is a *perfect* description of every single resident who comes to live at HIA. You don't get through treatment without realizing that you're already at the end of your rope—and that *that's* a blessing.

One of my favorite stories along these lines is the story of the amazing Shane Daugherty.

Shane's Story

"I was literally just living in a bedroom piled full of trash, with dirty needles everywhere, and an air mattress. I couldn't care less what happened outside of that room. As long as I was able to get a pill or get high that day, I could lie on that mattress and be totally happy."

That's Shane, talking now about the lowest point in his life. Of course, he wasn't "totally happy," but that's the way an addict thinks.

"By the time I hit my low," Shane says, "I was basically squatting in a house that I hadn't paid rent at in over a year. I slept on an air mattress. Every day, the only thing I cared about was getting high. Finding whatever drug I needed that day, whether it was heroin or Oxycontin, whatever opiate might be getting me high.

"I had nothing. I had pawned everything of value in my life, from guns to computers to tons of iPads, whether or not they were mine. Everything. I tried to pawn my car but they wouldn't take it. Everything of value was gone in my life, and that's not just monetary but relationships. That's my relationship with my parents, that's my relationship with my siblings. I had several people that I considered really good friends to me, who tried to do everything they could to help me, but I did them all wrong. My parents changed their locks. I wasn't allowed to go over there without them because I had stolen so much from them.

"I didn't have anything to contribute emotionally, conversationally, anything."

Shane was *definitely* at the end of his rope. Spaced out in a dirty home, on an air mattress, surrounded by needles and other drug paraphernalia… and not caring a single thing about it.

That's the end of your rope. Or, as we call it in this business, "rock bottom."

The thing is: no one really wants to find themselves here, but it's a must. Discovering what is rock bottom for you is crucial to getting your life turned around. So what did Shane's rock bottom look like? What motivated him off that air mattress and into the rest of his life?

" I showed up to my little brother's birthday party two hours late, just high as could be, nodding off. Just looked terrible. Embarrassed myself, embarrassed my family. Everybody left [and] there were a few other people there besides my family. I started talking to my mom and talking to my brother, and within the next few minutes, my entire immediate family was standing around me, talking to me about what they wanted for me and what I was capable of.

"They still knew me as that guy that was funny, and that was good at sports, and that had friends and all those things. But it wasn't the guy that I was anymore. I had lost all the characteristics that made me who I was.

"My sister said I had lost the entire essence of who I was as a person. And that's the fact. That's where I ended up. I ended up a completely different person that didn't have the intelligence, the personality, the soul that I had had just a few years before that.

"I just got to a point where I couldn't lower my standards anymore. I couldn't go any lower. And I realized that day that my life was in a very bad place.

"Having that conversation with my parents and my brothers and my sister—when you're out there using and doing drugs, all those people telling you that you need help, [you think] they're wrong. But for some reason, that night I knew that they were right. I knew I needed to do something, to change something."

Shane did change something. He went to treatment and started the long process of reframing his point of view. He started off just wanting to get off harder drugs but thinking that he could still use marijuana and hallucinogens. It took Shane awhile, but he finally was able to see that it wasn't about *not* using; it was about living the fullest, freest, most hope-filled life he could, something he began to catch when he moved into Hope Is Alive.

"My time at Hope Is Alive will always be looked back upon as some of the best years in my life. I was there for two years, and it was the time that I had one of the tightest, most close-knit groups of friends that I'll ever have. It was due not only to living in the same house, but we also did life together. We were together every night. We worked out together. We were doing meetings together. We ate together. We did *everything* together. And we loved each other!

"We were super-tight. That's one of the things that will always carry on with me. They're still my best friends. The guys I've lived with at Hope Is Alive are my best friends still to this day, years later. We still spend time together, go to the gym together, have dinners together."

Shane was at the end of his rope, but it just wound up being more room for God to establish His rule in Shane's life.

"Today my life is a thousand times better than I could have ever imagined. I'm moving forward and progressing in every area of my life. I have a great relationship with my family. I have a great relationship with my nephews. Before I sobered up, my nephew was a year old and I think I'd met him twice. Now I'm Uncle Shane. When I'm home with all the nephews, all you hear is 'Uncle Shane, Uncle Shane, Uncle Shane!' I'm able to be present with them today. To actually give them a piece of me. And that's a really amazing feeling. My career is back on track today as well. I'm happy. I'm productive. I get to live a life that I can be proud of today. To me, that's special, because not everybody gets that. 5½ years ago, I wouldn't have thought that was possible."

Shane's story is like so many other HopeDealer stories, and we're so grateful to have played a part in bringing it about. He's one of our "starting five," so he's been with us for awhile. He even saw HIA start to outgrow that original house.

#FOUR

FROM ONE TO TWO

"You're blessed when you feel you've lost what is most dear to you. Only then can you be embraced by the One most dear to you." (Matthew 5:4, MSG)

That first year of Hope Is Alive, things were going great. We had our Starting Five and everyone was completely on board with what we were doing. I had a lot of ideas on how the program should operate, all based on experience and training, and I was learning more and more. It was such a creative time for all of us as we, essentially, worked together to build this program from the ground up. We did a lot of experimenting (but not with drugs!), mainly because we were so idealistic and very much in the moment.

I wasn't thinking much—or at all—about the future. I was just focused on helping these guys and living life. And let's not forget: I wasn't that far into my own sobriety, so I was working this plan just as much as they were! But we graduated our first HopeDealer and just kept getting call after call after call from people who wanted what we had, who wanted to come live at Hope HQ.

One day I received a very unique call, not from someone looking for a home but from someone looking to rent one out. It was a guy I'd gone through treatment with. He had a house close to Hope HQ, and it was available for rent, and he needed some tenants quickly.

So what'd we do? We said YES! It was June 2014, and within thirty days we had five guys living there. We'd doubled in size almost overnight, and while it was exhilarating, it was also a little worrying. I had this great, core group of guys, all at Hope HQ, and I knew I could keep an eye on them and they on me, and now we had more men living in a totally different house. There was some of that unique, specialness gone. I'd lost a little something that was dear to me, but it gave God an opportunity to continue to push me outside of my comfort zone and closer to Him!

Many of our HopeDealers, and just people in general, have lost something or someone very dear to them, and so they turned to something to fill the void. But that only leaves them emptier.

Have you lost someone important to you? Did that threaten the stability of your world? Did you deal with that in a less-than-ideal way, lashing out against yourself or against those you love? Or maybe it wasn't a person but rather something else: money, or a home, or a career, or a marriage. Have you held the piercing pain of loss in the palm of your hand and tried to ignore it by sawing off your arm?

Perhaps you can relate, or perhaps not. Either way, I think you'll appreciate this: we had a couple of those guys come live in our second home who had experienced loss, and I want to tell you their stories now.

Tyler's Story

"My real father left when I was born, and I carried that around for a long time." The infant Tyler Barnes didn't yet know the Beatitude that said he's blessed when he feels he's lost what is most dear to him. How could he? And yet, that loss propelled him down a dark and lonely road.

"I didn't think I was good enough. I didn't think I belonged. I didn't think I fit in. I didn't think I was wanted, that's what it really boils down to. I didn't think I was wanted by the one person you want to want you. And because of that, I started to get into drug addiction as I went forward into high school. I still had those same feelings—I didn't feel like I was wanted by my peers, like I was wanted by anybody except for my mom."

Tyler's drug addiction took hold in adolescence and led him to link up with plenty of so-called friends who were absolutely not the kind of people that anyone would actually call a friend.

"I tried to get clean several times, and before I finally got clean, I relapsed. I overdosed and died. One minute I was alive, I was fine. I was shaking, trying to get high. And the next minute,

I was just waking up. I don't have any idea what's happening, what's going on. It's like you black out and lose time. And that's exactly what happened. It was a near-death experience. They tried to do CPR on me and I wasn't coming back. So this guy, my drug dealer, was trying to drag me through the window and was just going to call an ambulance and leave me out on the grass. But I just came back. Nobody knows why. It was like God just woke me up and said, 'All right, here's one more chance.'"

Tyler only had a nominal faith as a child and abandoned faith entirely when he dove headfirst into his drug use. "I'd always seen religion as a way to control people," Tyler says. "And when you look at Christianity, it's what really square people do. I'd never seen the practical side of it. I'd never experienced God. I'd never experienced that joy, that freedom, that hope. Life had always been pretty good and also I was a pretty good person here, selling heroin."

But it was faith that would eventually lead him to turn his life around. Not his own faith: his mom's.

"I attribute my desire to get clean to two things. One is mom's prayers. And the other is that, it says in scripture, 'If you raise up a child in the way he should go, when he is old he will not depart from it.' I don't think it says in scripture that he'll never depart from it, because for a time I did. I think part of it is the way my mom raised me, the way my mom loved me, the way my mom taught me about scripture.

"But the other thing is that she always had hope. She never

gave up on me, to the point where she knew God was going to do something. She believed it so much that she prayed for it. There were nights where she cried. I think it's probably her prayers that got me through some of those really dark moments. Moments where maybe I shouldn't have been breathing, moments where I should've been arrested and wasn't, moments where people had guns out and I didn't get shot. Things like that."

Ultimately Tyler went to treatment, but it was moving into that second Hope is Alive Home when he began to be embraced by the One most dear to him.

"At Hope Is Alive, I found a peace that was missing. I had a little bit of hope, but I hadn't experienced it. Hope is a journey. Hope is that first step. I'd taken that first step by the time I got there, because I'd found my relationship with Jesus, but I got to experience so much more. I got to experience real joy. I'd never truly experienced joy, and if you haven't ever experienced joy, it's one of those things that will take you off-guard.

"I remember when it happened. It transformed me. I thought, 'What is that feeling?' And it clicked that it was real joy and happiness.

"Another thing I found was peace of mind. As a drug addict, my mind was always going a million miles an hour. It was always thinking about the worst possible scenario. It was always in overdrive. Through Hope Is Alive, through working through the steps of recovery, I found a peace about myself, where I can just be alone by myself and be okay. Which is great, because I'm going through a time in my life where I'm alone about twelve hours a day, working on being a pastor, working through writing lessons, going to school, working from home. Because of that, I'm constantly alone, and I'm okay with that."

Tyler graduated from that second Hope is Alive Men's Home and continues to grow both in his life and in his walk with the Lord. Tyler is now married and is on staff at a local church, where he never misses a chance to share his hope with the people he gets to minister to.

"I tell them there are second chances. You can overcome what you're struggling with. We've all been wounded by something in life. We've all been damaged. But the great thing is: I'm not wounded anymore. I've been healed. There's a scar. That's what my drug addiction is—it's a scar on my life, but the thing about scars is that people get to see them and they want to hear the story behind them. I get to use that to point people towards my hope, which is Jesus Christ."

"If you look in Acts at Christian community and people doing life together, eating together, sharing their hopes, their fears, their struggles… that's what Hope Is Alive is. I got to laugh with people. I got to live with people. And just do life with people. I found my passion there, I found my purpose there. I learned how to prepare for my future. I'm still in a season of, I think, preparing me for what God really wants in my life, but that's where everything started. That's where the spark was ignited. That's my beginning. That's the first time I ever got to share with somebody that God had given me a purpose. It's the first place where I got to share my story. It's the first place where I got to do ministry. It's the first place where I got to tell someone about Jesus."

Christian's Story

Christian didn't lose a family member when he was a kid, but he did lose something important for every kid: a sense of belonging. Christian grew up in a strict household where the safest way to get by was to lay low and hope for the best.

"We were not a military family, but that's how the family was run," Christian says. "Every Saturday for us was waking up and doing yard work. If you wanted to go somewhere, you had to do something around the house. My dad was the type of person that, whatever happened around his friends, if he did not agree with the conversation they had, instead of showing them his true emotions, he would come home and show us. It was a fear-based environment.

"The way he taught us how to be a strong man, is how to take a whupping as a consequence for your actions. If he did not agree with what you did, you got a whupping. If you lost the fight and you came home, you got another whupping. It was what he relied on to correct us.

"He was very physically and emotionally abusive to us. He would talk down to us when he was angered, and he would make us feel lower than dirt. Sometimes I would rather take the physical abuse, because that would wear off after a day or two. But the emotional abuse was something that I carried on and later became an issue with me."

Christian lost the innocence of childhood but was not yet ready to be embraced by the One most dear to him. Christian spent his childhood seeking a way to find solace, and that led him to try pot when he was twelve years old.

"Pot was an eye-opener, it was a game-changer for me. Even though I didn't know the effects of marijuana, or had never experienced them, I liked the feeling. I noticed when I went home, and that tense environment was around me, I no longer was afraid. Nothing really bothered me. I was very relaxed. And so I kept smoking pot every day from that day on. It helped me cope with my situation."

It wasn't long before Christian drifted toward pain pills and, eventually, heroin. He wasn't yet out of his teenage years.

Christian's addiction progressed, and even though he began to make something like a life for himself, he still couldn't steer clear of trouble. He traded in the strictness of his father for the strictness of the legal system, landing in jail three times before finally heading to treatment to get sober at age 30. It was while in treatment that he heard about Hope Is Alive and decided that's where he needed to be.

"I came into Hope Is Alive very immature. I still had the mindset of a twelve-year-old. A little bit rebellious. I didn't know what to expect. All I knew was that whenever I saw the guys from HIA they were all laughing and seemed genuinely happy. I felt like I had to find out for myself how they got there. I was still a little bit troublesome when I got to HIA. The fact that I had true friends and brothers looking out for me without anything in return, that was something different and that's when everything began to change for me. I was able to get out of myself and start giving it a shot for the very first time. As I grew, I think it helped me mature a lot. They loved me when I couldn't love myself. They were able to help me with my confidence. They were able to help me forgive myself. They were very big on letting me know I was worth more than I thought I was.

"It was just a bunch of guys who wanted to see me do good, and that's all they wanted in return. Guys that I could have a deep, meaningful conversation and share some of my deepest, darkest secrets with, and they didn't judge me. People that just send me a text message during the day just to encourage me. And little by little they broke me down, and those guys have actually become more than just friends, they've become like family to me.

"These are people that I carry in my heart every day, and I don't think they realize how much they changed my life or what a difference they made in my life. I can honestly say I love them."

Christian found the sense of belonging that he never had as a kid, that environment where love wasn't earned and wisdom wasn't dispensed at the end of the lash. He found a place of hope, and it changed him completely. It turned him into a HopeDealer.

"Today I am an engaged man. I am a very loving and caring person. I'm a very understanding person. I'm a faithful person. I'm a person who has hopes and dreams that I know I can accomplish as long as I put the work in. I'm a person who has a brighter future. And hopefully one day I'll be a person who can change at least one life.

"I've learned a lot of things during my time at Hope Is Alive. I learned that everybody loves encouragement and everybody likes to be encouraged. I've learned what it is to be a leader. I've learned how to lead by example. I've also learned what it's like having true brothers and friendships outside of my family. I've learned how to handle my finances. I've learned what it is to be closer to God and search for Him. I've been able to learn that sobriety is fun, that you're able to still have a good time and have fun without having to alter your mind. I've learned what it is to love another person without having any walls up. How to handle my anger. How to help other people in need. And there's still a lot more to learn."

#FIVE

THE START OF THE NIGHT OF HOPE

"You're blessed when you're content with just who you are—no more, no less. That's the moment you find yourselves proud owners of everything that can't be bought." (Matthew 5:5, MSG)

We had two houses with ten guys and we were going strong. So what next? We were getting so many phone calls from parents who didn't know what to do with their drug-addicted son or daughter and we began to feel like God was calling us to help educate those parents—and really anyone—on where to go and where to turn for help in walking through their situation. And on top of that, as HopeDealers, we knew we needed to start spreading hope to our community. And so we decided to host a free event that we were going to call Night of Hope.

The idea: bring inspirational speakers to Oklahoma City, have some great music, tell some stories of lives being changed through Hope Is Alive and see what happens. We set a date, scheduled our speakers, and got the word out as best as we could, not expecting all that much of a turnout because, after all, we were a small, young organization with next to no name recognition.

We had 500 people.

That's a ton.

I was blown away!

So we knew that Night of Hope connected with folks and that it was something this area desperately needed. And we know that because we've continued to host Night of Hope gatherings all around Oklahoma and have to date seen almost 10,000 people come to them, and we've seen hundreds find treatment and get connected to support services and start living new lives. These events have become meaningful to the community, and not just to those in the community who need treatment.

One of the speakers we had at a couple of recent Night of Hope events was a woman named Ashley Smith Robinson. You may know her as the woman who was held hostage in Atlanta and who eventually wound up reading portions of *The Purpose-Driven Life* to her captor before convincing him to turn himself in to the authorities. Ashley wrote a book called *Unlikely Angel* about her story and recently sent me this very nice email about Night of Hope:

"Hope is Alive has become like a family to me. I have had the amazing opportunity to be part of 'A Night of Hope' on two separate occasions. Each time my life was blessed immensely. The nights not only brought hope to those around me but also brought hope to myself. I have been part of celebrating many events over the last 12 years of speaking and NO ONE does recovery like HIA. Their steps of 'doing life' produce positive, lasting change by starting with Jesus and continuing on daily by helping others start with Jesus. I am proud to call HIA part of my family."

But aside from that, Night of Hope has shown us here at Hope Is Alive the power of large community. We already knew the importance of small groups—that's the whole thought process behind our sober living homes, of course. Our homes crank out HopeDealers, but Night of Hope shows the power of putting all those HopeDealers together. People are desperate for hope. They're desperate for help. When you bring together a group of HopeDealers that big, people can find that hope and help, and then their lives can start to change for the better.

Things certainly changed for a young man named Blake Weiland, and I'd like to introduce you to him now.

Blake's Story

"I think from the start, I felt as if I wasn't enough. Parents and family and everyone in my life would tell me, 'You're a great person, you can be anything you want to be,' but I felt like I wasn't enough. Everyone else would see me score a run in baseball, and I would think, 'There are ten guys who are better than me.' I'm average at this, I'm average at that. I felt like I wasn't adequate enough in life."

Blake is anything but average, and you can tell that from the moment you meet him. But the way we see ourselves often doesn't line up with the way others see us, and Blake was a textbook example of that. It really came to a head after he graduated from high school and went off to college.

"I remember feeling very lonely the first two months of college. I was pretty isolated. It seemed to be what everyone else was doing."

"I remember from the first time, after having a couple of drinks, walking across the street to the party that we were attending, and thinking, 'Ah, this is why people drink alcohol. This is that feeling. This is what it does.' And the next morning when I woke up, I had all these new friends. Everyone wanted to get together and share stories. The guy who lived down the hall from me, that I had nothing in common with? We were now good buddies. It was that unity, that subconscious hole that I always had was filled, so to speak. I fit in."

"Alcohol also gave me false confidence from the first time. I thought I was better looking. Thought I was smoother talking. Thought I was funnier. Every decent quality I thought I had was improved whenever I drank, whenever I was under the influence of substances."

Blake was initially a very high-functioning drinker, so he still excelled in school, gradually increasing his alcohol intake until one day he suffered a panic attack, his hands shaking violently, and discovered that booze made that go away. He spent the next four months with a drink constantly nearby.

Knowing the situation wasn't tenable but not really knowing what else to do about it, Blake reluctantly attended a Night of Hope with his parents.

"I was living at home, at the mercy of my parents, and I knew I was putting them through a lot. My dad came to me one morning and said, 'I know you don't want to go, but this Friday there's a thing in Oklahoma City that your mother and I want to take you to.' I had no idea if this was treatment or a Bible study group or to talk to a counselor or what. He said, 'I found it in the newspaper. It's called Night of Hope.' And I said, 'Yeah, I'll do that.' So we went.

"Upon arriving, it's the greeting. Everybody is so happy to be there. And I think at first, it was like, 'Oh, I gotta pretend like I'm happy, I gotta pretend like everything's going well in my life!' Little did I know: those greeters were addicts. Those were people who'd been through what I'd been through. I didn't understand that.

"I walked into a full sanctuary there at Quail Springs Baptist Church, and I think I sat next to a guy who was 12, right next to a woman who looked like she was about 85. They were both there, and I don't think I realized they had problems of their own. It was very emotional. There was a time that was dedicated to the parents, specifically the mothers, and I think that was a good time for me to realize all I had put them through. It was very uplifting and positive, and I think that put a seed in my brain for later.

"I wasn't ready to quit then, but I had that experience in my mind, for whenever I was ready to quit. I knew I couldn't go on drinking, and I certainly knew I couldn't quit, and that's a really bad place to be."

Night of Hope did indeed put a seed in Blake's brain, and three months later when he was ready to do what it took to get and maintain his sobriety, he entered treatment and while there, he saw a familiar face.

"The first evening in treatment, they bring in host meetings. These may be outside treatment centers, outside programs, and the first one, the first night I was there, was Hope Is Alive. And, across the room, there's that Lance Lang guy that I saw four months prior at Night of Hope. He talked about how there's no idea what the Lord's going to do with you if you just give him 2% of your trust. I talked with Lance afterward and he told me that I was a leader and that God was going to do amazing things with my life, so buckle up because it was going to be a crazy ride. And from that moment I knew I wanted a bed in Hope Is Alive."

I can't get over this story, that an idea I had several years before I even knew Blake wound up having such a huge impact on him. Night of Hope changed his life and, as a result, changed the lives of those around him. His family, his siblings, his future wife... all of them changed by Night of Hope.

You never know what God can do when you say YES. In

the case of Night of Hope, we felt a sense of calling and obeyed that sense. It was a lot of work but it was the right thing to do, and we've since heard hundreds of stories like Blake's that have arisen from seeds that were planted during a Night of Hope.

It's just part of being a HopeDealer. What would happen if you were obedient to living out your story and saying YES to the calling that God has placed on your life? Not all HopeDealers put on big community events—that was something God called us to do here at Hope Is Alive. What is God calling *you* to do? What is He asking *you* to say YES to? Maybe you don't need to host events that will reach 10,000 people—maybe you just need to host a dinner at your home. Maybe you need to start speaking your story to those friends of yours at church who are sure you have it all together. Maybe you need to share your life with others who have a story similar to yours.

Maybe it's time to become a HopeDealer. It's never too late to start.

#SIX

FROM TWO TO THREE

"You're blessed when you've worked up a good appetite for God. He's food and drink in the best meal you'll ever eat." (Matthew 5:6, MSG)

While our Nights of Hope were ministering to people in the community, our profile was growing and our phone was ringing off the hook (not really of course, because we all have smartphones, which don't have hooks, but "our phones were buzzing off the table" doesn't have the same ring to it).

We knew we were going to need to add a third house. We had calls coming in not just from the Oklahoma City area or even just Oklahoma in general, but from all over the country. As much as we HopeDealers want to say YES, sometimes we do have to tell people "not yet." We wanted to grow but we wanted to do it in a wise way so that we didn't grow faster than we could handle. So much of Hope Is Alive has worked out because we waited to do things in God's timing. We keep our ears inclined toward Him in anticipation so that when He says "Go" we're ready to respond with our YES. We had to wait for such a time as this, and we knew that now was the right time.

We started looking around for a new house and found yet another one that was very close to Hope HQ, the original home. I wish I had a sexy story about God's provision falling out of the sky and constructing a home for us out of manna, but that's just not what happened. A lot of times HopeDealers walk in supernatural provision and have cool stories full of confirmation about how God took care of them in a spectacular way. But when it comes to the story of this third home, all the juice is telling about the people who lived there, not in getting the home itself. That's okay. HopeDealers can embrace the mundane just as much as the miraculous.

So getting the home? That was mundane. The people who came to us, though? Those were the miracles. And two of those miracles are named Colin and Zach.

Colin's Story

"When I was a kid growing up, I had a disease called autoimmune hepatitis and I also have common variable immunodeficiency, where I don't have my full immune system. So I can easily get sick, and when I do, it's a lot worse for me because I don't have an immune system to fight it off. This affected my childhood because I wasn't allowed to do a lot of things or I would get sick and miss a lot of school, or my mom would be more cautious of me around different situations. My other disease was where my body attacked my liver and treated it like a transplant liver, so I was on the same medications that transplant patients were on."

Despite being on all these medications, Colin was a good kid who had plenty of positive peer interactions throughout childhood.

"I feel like I had some great teenage years. I had all the friends I wanted, I was involved in everything at school, I got good grades, I was able to go to college, I got into every college I applied to, I didn't have a lot of heartache. I didn't really feel heartache until my senior year in college. Before that, I had a pretty picture-perfect life.

"My senior year of college, my dad and my mom split up. It came out of nowhere. My dad drove down to Norman where I was living with some friends, and he told me he was driving home to tell my mom he was moving out.

"It hit me like a ton of bricks. I hadn't been in the house for three or four years, so I didn't know what was going on there. I was all about myself throughout college, as many kids are. They're removed and only worried about what's in front of them.

"It just so happened that I had begun to experiment with pills right around the same time, so it was kind of the perfect storm. I started to feel actual emotional pain for the first time. And there happened to be a substance around that I could use that numbed that pain to the point where I didn't feel it.

"The emotional pain turned into physical pain, like an anxious feeling in your chest that you just couldn't get out. Drugs eliminated that. I wouldn't feel that stomach feeling, that pain, that feeling where I wanted to throw up all the time. But when I would lay down in bed and be still, I would feel that at night, when I was just sitting alone.

"I wanted to feel nothing and drugs allowed me to. I was in college, so I was removed from anyone that was really looking out for me. I was still making good grades, so no one had any reason to think they needed to come check in on me.

"I was using Adderall and downers, so I was taking pills to get through the day and then taking pills to go to sleep. So I was high getting my schoolwork done during the day and then high going back down to sleep. It was just different variations of being high. Constantly medicated, 24/7.

"Drugs were really cool at the beginning. I thought the Adderall equaled success, because I was doing well in school. It started out not as a drug for me but just a way to make good grades. Then I became dependent on that drug to make good grades. In my mind I felt that if I was not taking Adderall, then I was not studying to my full potential, so it became a crutch, a necessity."

Colin felt an intense pressure to perform academically, tying his identity first of all to his scholastic achievements and then, upon graduating from college, to whatever job he would be able to land.

"I went to six years of school and had nothing to show for it. I did my undergrad and my master's in accounting, and at the end of all that, I didn't have a job. And it wasn't because I wasn't smart; it was because I was not capable of being a good employee because of the drug use. That was kind of where rock bottom was. No job, no idea of what was going to come in the future. I had nothing going for me."

Colin's story is why I love the Beatitude that goes with this chapter, because he wasn't yet content with just who he was. Colin always felt the pressure both from those around him and from within, and that pressure drove him to prescription drugs.

We know we have an enemy and that enemy seeks to devour us. In this case, the enemy fed Colin a lie about who he was so that Colin could continue to wallow in debilitating circumstances for years or even for the rest of his life.

But God had a bigger, better plan. He always does.

"Hope started settling probably a month into rehab. My head started to clear, I started to gain weight, I started looking more normal. I started being able to see myself again and being able to see God. And when I say 'see God,' my journey with God was not instantaneous. I just tried to start seeking Him, and it took a long time. It's not something that would happen overnight, but I know *now* that He was watching over me *then*.

"My journey into the Hope Is Alive program was not like most people's journeys. They came down my last week of rehab and suggested I go to sober living, and while it wasn't something

I'd really planned on, I wasn't closed off to the idea either.

"I got into the house and I didn't meet Lance for the first week I was there because he was out of the country, but I could tell it was going to be a great fit. I got in and within six months I was a house manager. It fit me perfectly. God had His hand on me. He brought me to Hope Is Alive and I ended up staying a year and a half."

Through Hope Is Alive, Colin was able to get a clean start and to begin developing an understanding of who he really was—and that was a person he was able to be content with. But he wasn't ready right away to accept the fact that that discovery was going to be a process.

"Getting out of rehab, I wanted to get my life back *immediately*. I wanted to be working in an accounting firm or somewhere, making big money, striving for success as I knew it at that time, which was money, power, status, house, car. God had a different plan for me. He had to humble me and figure out a way to break me down a bit.

"That first three or four months out of rehab, I actually had to settle for a construction job. That's not where I wanted me to be, but it's where God needed me to be to teach me about hard work, about money management, about what was really important in life. To teach me that money and status were not what He wanted me to be striving for, what He wanted my life to be driven by. He had to take that away, and I gradually got it back. I started working for an oil company, and then for a bank, and now I'm with another bank. It was a progression of better jobs and better jobs and better jobs. I had to get everything back on God's time, not on my own time. I had to learn to wait."

He had to learn to wait. Sound familiar? It reminds me of a certain psalmist who wrote a certain HopeDealer verse: "I waited patiently for the Lord to help me, and he turned to me and heard my cry." Colin did some patient waiting on God, but, though he didn't know it, God was doing some patient waiting on *Colin*.

"When I moved into Hope Is Alive, they gave an emphasis on finding Jesus and going to church, that Jesus was the way to a fulfilling life. It really took me a year of sober living before I started actually being able to feel the presence of the Lord. Not feeling like I was just praying to the ceiling, but being able to see His imprint on my life.

"It wasn't osmosis that this happened, it was me, in Hope Is Alive, continually pursuing, even though I didn't feel like I was getting any results. It finally started to click. But there was a year where I went to church every week and I prayed and I tried to read my Bible as much as I could possibly remember to every day, and not feeling like anything was different. It really took a year."

A long year, to be sure, but a year where Colin was able to find, at the end of it, that he owned something that couldn't be bought.

Zach's Story

"From the outside looking in, it appeared we had a pretty run-of-the-mill family, pretty functional family, but the reality was far different. I grew up with an alcoholic father, and that played a big role in my upbringing. He wasn't really present in my childhood. It was more bringing home money to support the family. It was kind of my mom, my sister, my brother, and us on our own. He'd often come home drunk late at night. He was unfaithful to my mom. All of that stuff affected me a lot growing up, so I looked elsewhere for that father figure.

"Early on I found that father figure in my grandpa, my Papa Joe. He taught me a lot of life lessons, a lot of great stuff. But when I was eight years old, my grandpa passed away from leukemia, and that hit me hard.

"I can remember being angry at God for taking my grandpa away so soon and asking questions of why? Why did this happen to him? Why did it happen to a good person like him? That affected me a lot, probably as much as my dad being an alcoholic. I began to turn away from God and walk away from God. I spent a lot of time playing basketball, trying to find outlets other than family, other than God, to fill that hole I had within.

"I felt like I was always looking, searching for my dad's approval. He was finding fulfillment in the bottle. I wanted the approval of my father but I couldn't find that just from conversations with him. That's why I spent countless hours playing basketball. Practicing basketball. Because he recognized when I performed well on the basketball court. When I had a lot of friends, if I was popular, then he would recognize that. So I searched in those outlets for approval from my dad.

"By my senior year, my parents were separated and living in different homes until they eventually divorced. When my parents separated, I started to drink with my dad. I thought that was cool. He recognized me when I drank with him. I got his approval when I'd drink with him. I would throw parties at his house, and he'd be passed out on the couch drunk by midnight while my friends and I kept partying throughout the night.

"I didn't realize that wasn't normal. I thought everybody had a dad who drank all the time. I thought that was cool, that my dad was the cool dad. I thought it was cool that I was drinking with my dad.

"As his alcoholism progressed, it got embarrassing, to the point where he was living at this nasty house. I got the idea to take some friends over there one time and it was just a pit. Alcohol bottles everywhere. It was embarrassing. In that moment, I thought, 'This isn't cool anymore. I don't want to be like that.' But I definitely became that. The one person I didn't want to become, I did become."

Things spiraled downward quickly for Zach. He went off to college and fell into a major party lifestyle, supplementing his mammoth alcohol intake with progressively harder drugs, eventually dealing so that he could support his habit. Even still, he was able to keep up his GPA and was doing relatively well in school… until he was arrested for selling drugs and drug paraphernalia. That led to him being suspended from school for a year, and that hit hard.

"I began to experiment with prescription painkillers. I moved out of my dad's house and in with a buddy, and my addiction continued to get worse. It started out with Lortabs, then Oxycodone. I was popping them and then snorting them and then eventually shooting them. I became an IV drug user."

Things were getting progressively worse for Zach. His father had gone into treatment and was successfully working a program of sobriety, but Zach wasn't willing to follow his dad's lead. Fortunately for Zach, he had a family full of HopeDealers who weren't going to give up on him.

"It was January 6, 2015. The week prior, I'd been reaching out to my mom, telling her I was willing to go to treatment. But then I'd back out. I was at home, trying to detox on my own. I was lying in bed when I heard someone come in the house. I thought that was weird, so I went downstairs and it was my dad, my grandma, and my sister. My dad looked at me—there was paraphernalia strewn about the house, bongs, pills, everything— and he said, 'If you don't come with me to detox, then I'm going to call the police on you.'"

But that wasn't enough to motivate Zach to leave that home and go into treatment. No, it wasn't until his sister got vulnerable that his eyes opened.

"What convinced me that I needed to get help in that

intervention was looking at my sister in the eyes, tears running down her face, telling me that she didn't want to see her older brother die. It was in that moment that I realized I needed to get some help. It was the darkest day of my life, and through the tears coming down my sister's eyes, I saw a flicker of hope. I saw light in the darkness.

"It was my sister believing in me when I didn't believe in myself, and her having faith in me when a lot of people had given up on me. I really believe that, if it wasn't for her, there's a good chance I wouldn't have gotten the help and that I wouldn't be here today."

HopeDealers, you never know when the truth will break through. That's why you have to keep telling it, over and over.

You've probably figured out by now, of course, that Zach came to us at Hope Is Alive, and from the time I met him, I knew this man was destined to be a huge leader for us. Today, he's discipling men. He's leading groups. He's mentoring people. Zach found the love he was looking for and now he's content with exactly who he is. 100%. Zach is the embodiment of a HopeDealer.

"What blows my mind about my life today is that I get the opportunity to sit down and talk with men who are on the same path as me. I get to share my story in churches, which is just nuts. I write sometimes now, and I enjoy that. I think today I'm finally fulfilling that purpose that God put on my heart years ago, fulfilling that calling. I think I've always wanted to help people.

"I think back to a time when I was still in my addiction, and I was sitting there with a friend of mine. We were talking, and she asked me, 'Zach, what's our purpose on this earth? What are we here for?' I thought about it for a little bit and I told her that I think that if I could positively impact one person's life, then it would all be worth it. The cool thing is that today I'm getting to live out that purpose. I'm getting to help people. More than one! It's crazy how I've been given this opportunity in order to share the hope that I've found."

If you've had a tough life, I'm going to guess that you also have a toughness about you, a resilience, and that means you have great power to help others. Our enemy knows that! He doesn't want you to help people! He wants you to keep believing the lie that you'll never be content, never be satisfied, never be fulfilled.

But the HopeDealer knows who they are. They're grounded in Christ and are owners of everything that can't be bought. They know they'll never run out of hope and so they give it freely to everyone they encounter.

Both Zach and Colin are completely sold out to the Lord and they're great examples of giving back. They're out there sharing their stories with anyone who will listen. They're bringing a culture of being excited and engaged with Jesus, from digging into daily devotionals to being completely captivated with going to church on Sunday morning.

They're miracles, plain and simple. They're HopeDealers.

#SEVEN

THERE IS HOPE TO FIND

"You're blessed when you care. At the moment of being 'care-full,' you find yourselves cared for." (Matthew 5:7)

One thing I discovered as we began to hold more Night of Hope events and began to take more and more phone calls from people around the country was that there were a lot more people needing help than just men in recovery. Specifically, God started putting it on my heart to start offering some kind of resource for parents and spouses of addicts. Again, this is something that HopeDealers do: we look for areas where we can engage. So I knew this was something that needed to happen, but I also knew, like so much of what we were doing with HIA, that it needed to happen in God's time.

Things were progressing well with Hope Is Alive. I'd written and published my first two books, while more and more speaking opportunities were opening up at churches farther and farther afield from Oklahoma City. Which is how I wound up telling my story one Sunday morning at Canadian Valley Baptist Church in Yukon, Oklahoma. After the service, I had the great honor of speaking with different members of the congregation as they approached me, and one woman really leapt out.

As I had been telling my story that morning, I'd noticed this particular woman in the crowd. I could tell she was dealing with a lot of pain all through the service, holding back emotionally, though with tears in her eyes. When she came to me afterward, that dam broke. She wept as she told me about how she and her husband had recently lost their son to addiction. She had heard that I was going to be speaking that day, so while her husband had to fulfill responsibilities at another church, she'd come on her own to hear what I'd have to say. Her name is Tanya Dorris, and I had no idea that she and her husband Mike were about to become inextricably intertwined with Hope Is Alive.

Mike and Tanya took HIA and, by extension, me under their wing. They showed me the most incredible kindness, making lunches for me and sending me cards on my birthday. We became great friends, but what I didn't know was that during this whole season, God was putting the same HopeDealer story in both of us at the same time.

See, because of their experience with their son, Mike and Tanya were really wanting to help HIA develop a support group for parents and spouses of addicts, too. They were letting that vision develop within them at the same time it was developing within me, until one day they set up a lunch appointment with me. They told me about their heart and I smiled as I told them I had the same heart.

It wasn't long before we were sitting with their pastor to pitch him this idea, and it also wasn't long before we hosted our first Finding Hope class at that pastor's church, Putnam City Baptist Church.

We didn't advertise it much. We launched it without a whole lot of fanfare. And yet the people came. From the very first day, we outgrew the classroom we had reserved. We packed 35 people into this hot, small, cramped room and met Jesus. There were people sitting next to each other who had attended the same church for years and had never known they each had sons who were struggling with drugs.

We've had so many powerful moments since then. People have made their way into treatment and then into our homes. People have found out they aren't alone. People have found that hope isn't dependent on circumstances. We have classes meeting in both Oklahoma City and Tulsa, and many more are starting up in other parts of this country. Hundreds of people have attended Finding Hope and thousands of lives have been touched because I spoke at a small church in Yukon, Oklahoma and Tanya and Mike opened their hearts up to God and said YES.

This is so powerful! We've heard so many marvelous, encouraging stories that have emerged from Finding Hope, but none have impacted me quite like the two I'm about to tell you.

Cindy F.'s Story

"I never did have any issues with drugs or alcohol, thank God. I didn't. It's not something I ever thought about with my kids. I just didn't. They were great kids. They still are. In fact, I remember having a conversation with my husband at the time about our son, saying, 'You know, I just don't think we'll ever have to worry about drugs or alcohol with him.' He was a tae kwon do national competitor. Trained five, six days a week. I said, 'However, I think we need to have the sex talk with him, because he's handsome.' Girls liked him. He liked girls. Not until his senior year did I become aware that drugs were a part of his life.

"Riley came home from a skate night that the school had had. I met him in the laundry room, and I could smell it. For starters, he had somebody else's pants on. So that was kind of a, 'Well, what's up? Where are your pants?' You can imagine how it went from there. I didn't freak out. I was concerned, but that was the very first time ever."

Cindy's son Riley had a problem, and she didn't know what to do. She didn't yet know the word "enablement" and so she did her best to care for her son in the best way she knew how. After a long battle with addiction and three arrests, he agreed to go to treatment and even to a sober living home. But, unfortunately for Riley, the allure of his old life began to draw him back.

"It was a couple of years after treatment that he started exhibiting the same signs, and I knew things weren't great. I didn't know to what extent, but I'd learned enough to know that something was up. He was arrested for a *fourth* time. The good news is, he did not call me to bail him out."

Cindy is a hair stylist, and the next day she was sitting with a regular client and struck up the usual conversation. Her client suggested that she attend a parent support group meeting for an organization that does work similar to Finding Hope. The meeting was that night, and after wrestling with it for a short while, Cindy finally decided it was time to visit.

"I was scared to death because I didn't know what was going to happen to Riley. He was still on probation on an eight-year deferred sentence. I cancelled my last two appointments and drove to Edmond, Oklahoma, to this meeting. I sat by myself on the back row, and they said that this guy Lance Lang was going to be the speaker. I heard Lance's story. I cried the entire time, but for the first time ever, I felt like there was some help for *me*. I went to that meeting for *myself*, not for Riley, and that was a first."

"I'm so grateful Lance talked about his story and about the importance of loved ones taking care of themselves. Afterwards I went up and met Lance. I told him about Riley and asked him to pray for him. That was really the beginning of my journey of recovery, and I didn't even know I had a recovery journey! I didn't know. I'm just the mom. As a mom, you just listen and pay and drive and pick up and make phone calls… and fall apart and lose yourself. Sometimes lose your marriage, lose your health, lose your finances. Get behind at work. Lose your relationship with your other children because you're so focused on this child.

"Now I know that I cannot fix Riley. It's not my place to. And because I know now exactly, looking at this from a spiritual aspect, what the enemy is trying to do to my son, that's just the tip of the iceberg. He wants my son, he wants my marriage, he wants to destroy my health, my finances. And I've learned through some personal study and Finding Hope meetings that I have a choice! I can just let him or not. And I'm choosing 'not.'"

Through Finding Hope, Cindy learned that she was so much more than just Riley's Mom. She learned that *her* story matters. That she needs to care for herself just as much as she needs to care for her family, and part of caring for herself is caring about her story. Cindy now comes to Finding Hope with a friend, always looking and listening for someone who needs what she has found. HopeDealers are always on the lookout for someone they can impact, and Finding Hope has turned Cindy into a HopeDealer. Which leads me to another story about another Cindy.

Cindy L.'s Story

"My college sweetheart that I married is a great guy, otherwise I wouldn't have married him. We had two sons and they're fine young men today, they're 33 and 32. I've been teaching all these years, but we also had a hunting business on the side. And over the years, people would bring in their alcoholic drinks into this business in Texas. And in a process of 20 years of that, my husband became an alcoholic. I'm not blaming the people who came into our business; this is a choice he made. In 2004, we were divorced, not particularly because of the drinking, but because of the lifestyle that he lived and the choices that he made. He wanted out of the marriage.

"I moved to Oklahoma and it was the worst time in my life. I was still willing to fight for my marriage, but my ex was not. I just didn't understand. I was brought up with no drinking. I was really never around it. I didn't know why someone would drink in excess and not be able to control themselves or to throw their family away. I did seek counseling, and the counselor suggested I go to Al-Anon meetings to educate myself on alcoholism, so I did.

"Those were a little tough for me. I didn't like that they called it a 'higher power'. I struggled with that because I knew that was God. So I'd just say 'God'. And these sweet ladies were talking about this disease. I just thought, 'It's not a disease. You choose to put that drink in your mouth and you can choose not to put it in your mouth.' So I didn't go back. I thought I was really smart, smarter than the wisdom that was sitting around that table. I didn't have a clue at that point."

Through continued counseling, Cindy began to find forgiveness for her ex-husband, and things began to look up for her until, about a year later, she met the man who would become her husband, Doug.

"Doug is actually an old friend, and he was not someone I

thought I would ever marry, or even be interested in. I wasn't going to go looking. I told the Lord, 'If you want me to be with someone, you're going to have to bring them to my door.' And that's exactly what happened! Doug came to my door one day, just as an old friend. We were reacquainted and were friends for awhile. He is a very genuine, loving, kind, humble—very humble—person. Long story short, I fell in love with him and we were married in 2006. It wasn't a very long engagement. And I'm married to him today! He is a great man.

"Before Doug and I were married, he told me he'd had a drinking problem in the past. And he knew my past, how hurtful the drinking had been, and told me that would never be part of his life again, that that was a problem he had struggled with but that he would never go there again and he would never, ever hurt me.

"Things were great for some time. And then Doug started drinking. I was totally shocked. I thought, 'What in the world have I done?' And then I thought, 'Why did I marry two men that drink? What's wrong with me that I would do this again?'"

This began a cycle of recovery and relapse in Doug's life, which, of course, greatly affected Cindy's life. She began her own cycle of despondency which corresponded with Doug's cycle, and the hope slowly began to drain out of her world.

And here's where I need to mention that I had a personal connection to Cindy. See, to me, she's not "Cindy," she's "Mrs. Lacefield," because not only had she come to my church when I was a kid, but at one point she was my children's schoolteacher. And not only that: she was their teacher when I was in the worst phase of *my* addiction. Sadly, I never met her while my children were her students. But because of our connections, she'd heard that I had gotten clean. And because of all *that*, when the world of social media began to ensnare all of us in its net, Cindy and I became Facebook friends, where she began to read all my ramblings about Hope Is Alive and the encouragements that I often post.

"I admired Lance and was so proud of him for turning his life around and for the things he was doing for these other men. Then he posted that he wanted to start doing classes for families of addicts. I read that and thought, 'This may be me. I grew up with a brother who had struggled, gone through it with my ex, and now I'm with my husband. I should do this.'

"A good friend called me and told me that her son was struggling with an addiction, and though I knew he had a few problems, I didn't realize how much he'd been struggling. She had seen on Facebook about this Finding Hope class at this church in Oklahoma City, and I told her I'd seen the same post. So I said, 'If you'll go, I'll go.' It was just the encouragement that I needed.

"I remember walking up that sidewalk and just praying the Lord would help me get through this, help me to walk in, help me to be what I needed to be. Help me open my mind so I could hear what I needed to hear. And I did! I'll never forget the couple at the door. They just had warm, kind faces, and, I came to find out later, they'd lost their son to addiction. Then I came around the corner and there was Lance. I gave him a hug and thought, 'I can do this. There's a friendly face.' I cried a lot that evening.

"For the very first time, what I walked out with that night was, 'You have to take care of yourself.' I remember thinking when I first went in, 'They're going to fix Doug.' But Lance said, 'We're not here to fix the addict. We're in this class, and I'm here to encourage you as a family member of the addict. I'm here for *you*.' I really hadn't held that thought. It hadn't been about me. I didn't need fixing. I was okay. But for the first time, at the first meeting, when Lance said I had to take care of myself before I could help the addict, it just clicked with me. This *is* about me."

Cindy kept coming to Finding Hope and is now one of our most stalwart attendees.

"I have learned in these classes that I have a ministry to other people who are hurting. I know we'll see the big picture in heaven, but what did I miss out on by not telling the truth sometimes or hiding Doug's addiction or not sharing with people because of pride or because I didn't know what they were going to think about my husband? But now, because of Finding Hope classes, I openly share with people.

"I'm living a life of thankfulness. I haven't always lived there, but I truly live in thankfulness now. Because when you've lived on the other side, even a couple of years ago, when you're down in that valley, there is nothing like the feeling that comes when you reach the mountaintops. So I'm thankful for what God has carried me through, and I'm thankful that I can openly tell others about it, so that God *can* use me. If I'm honest, then God can use me. If I let the pride go and just say, 'Okay, Lord. I am who I am. You know my story. Just use me!"

I get so pumped seeing both of these Cindys and knowing how much of an impact they're having on their worlds by embracing their lives as HopeDealers and telling their stories. So many parents and spouses are finding freedom and health because they now know they aren't alone. That's the joy of dealing hope. You can care for others and get cared for yourself at the same time.

#EIGHT

INSIDE AND OUTSIDE

"You're blessed when you get your inside world—your mind and heart—put right. Then you can see God in the outside world." (Matthew 5:8, MSG)

This particular Beatitude is such a tough one. I think a lot of us want to look at the outside world first and try to get that "put right." I know I see this a lot in our Finding Hope groups. These are people who love addicts—of course they want to put those addicts right! I've been doing this work a long time, and even *I'm* tempted to think along those lines.

But the fact of the matter is that it's so very crucial for us to get our minds and hearts put right before we can do anything else. And this reality is not limited to the Beatitudes either. In fact, I'd say we see a form of this just three verses into the Bible.

"In the beginning God created the heavens and the earth. The earth was formless and empty, and darkness covered the deep waters. And the Spirit of God was hovering over the surface of the waters." (Genesis 1:1-3)

God wants to create in our lives, and I believe this creation story is a window into God's creation process. Creation starts with the Spirit hovering. And then, when the time is right, God speaks and light floods the world and the creation is on.

I believe God is hovering over us now, all of us, just waiting for the right time. He's hovering, nudging us, urging us, guiding us, directing us to get our hearts and minds right. And then, when the time is right, He speaks to us.

I believe God is hovering, listening for those of you who are ready to say YES. Whose hearts and minds have come into alignment with His will and His word so that He can take our YES and turn it into something that breathes new life into this world that He is still actively creating.

But we must recalibrate our minds. You can't fix anyone—not even yourself—until you have your mind and heart put right, recalibrated to line up with how God works.

Tripping a few pages further into scripture, I think about Moses and how he wanted to do the right thing but he went about it the wrong way. Even though he'd been raised by an Egyptian princess, Moses knew he was an Israelite, so when he saw a fellow Israelite being mistreated by an Egyptian, he murdered the tormenter as a way of setting that Israelite free. But that wasn't what God had in store for him! He had limited vision, so he couldn't yet see God at work in the outside world. Moses just needed to chill in Midian for a while, get married, have some kids, and *then* experience God in the Burning Bush before leading the Israelites out of Egypt in a massive exodus.

Or what about Samson? Here's a guy who knew how to flex and show off the power of God—but with none of the heart. He instead made a bunch of wrong, fleshly choices that led to him being thrown down from his high position as a judge of Israel and instead captured by his enemies, blinded, shaved, and completely and utterly reduced to a shell of his former self. Ironically, it was when Samson was blinded that he was able to see God in the outside world. That was when he humbled himself, prayed for strength, and brought down the pillars of a pagan temple as a final testament to God.

Or what about Saul? Not the Israelite king of the Old Testament but the devout Israelite of the New Testament. He thought his mind and heart were right about all these people following after this Jesus guy. He thought that God wanted to blot the Christians off the face of the earth. He thought he was right but it took a literal vision from Jesus Himself for Saul to become Paul and see that God had been working in the outside world all along—and that He'd done it specifically through Jesus.

And then I think of a couple of HopeDealers that have come our way. First up, Jim and Karen Myers.

The Story of Jim and Karen

Jim and Karen are a wonderful older couple who have gotten very involved in Finding Hope. But their story has a twist: they found one another very late in life, getting married in 2010. Jim had no children, but Karen had three, including her son David. He's the reason they came to Finding Hope.

"We had a conservative Christian home and David was raised that way," Karen says. "He was a good student, made good grades in grade school, middle school, high school. He made good scores on his SAT and ACT and was accepted into Colorado School of Mines right out of high school.

"The first semester he did pretty well, but he started meeting fraternity people and getting invited to parties, and that's where he started drinking. Being as far away from him as I was, living in Oklahoma City, I wasn't aware of how bad the drinking was until he called me one day and said, 'My counselor suggested I withdraw from school while I'm passing.'"

David's path included a series of jobs, a marriage, a miscarriage, a divorce, and stays in several different cities from Colorado to Oklahoma to Arizona before coming back to Oklahoma City to attempt a new start, though that was still fueled by alcohol.

Doing the best they could to try to help David stay on the level, Jim and Karen supported him the only way they knew how.

"We had enabled to a certain degree because of his jobs," Jim says. "One was as an insurance salesman for AFLAC, so we thought, 'Okay, we can justify buying a policy for each of us.' And then he lost that job. Then he got a job doing sales for a roofing company, and he seemed to be doing well. We thought, 'We could stand to get a new roof,' so we bought a roof from him. Not long after that, he lost that job for the same reasons. And then the third job was a very good job selling windows, high-quality windows. He was doing quite well at it, and it turned out that if we were to buy some windows, it would push him way over his highest profit compensation ability, so, sure enough, we bought many thousands of dollars' worth of windows. And it wasn't too long after that that we found out he lost that job as well."

"I thought I was helping him," Karen says. "I thought, 'If we get him groceries now, then he'll eat and feel better and go back to work. If we pay this bill off, then he can catch up on his bills and continue to be on his own. If we get him a car, he can drive to his job instead of having to walk or take a bus, or say he's not going to work because he didn't have a car.' We paid his rent from time to time."

Jim and Karen were growing increasingly frustrated and despondent with David, eventually feeling like they needed to cut all ties with him. But their inside world was still tangled up with bad information, and it wasn't until they came to Finding Hope after seeing me speak that they found the confirmation they needed to follow through on what they'd already thought.

"We came to the very first class of Finding Hope," Karen

says. "We learned that it was a disease. We learned that we needed to set some boundaries. Right away, we began to discuss what that was going to look like. We met with David, hoping that he would be somewhat sober at the time, and told him that we could no longer help him in any way, emotionally, financially, or anything. Nothing. Not that we didn't still love him, not that we wouldn't continue to pray for him. We couldn't assist him or enable him any longer. And this class gave us confidence to do that."

It wasn't easy, but Jim and Karen did what they felt was right.

"After we started coming to Finding Hope, and he didn't speak to us for about six months, David detoxed himself and started going to AA meetings," Karen says. "It still was another two or three months before he contacted us and started sharing some of his success stories. He's at a point in his life he's never been. He's allowed God to guide and direct his thoughts and his plans, he went for his PRSS certification, and he's now currently working in a state job that gives back. He's working specifically with homeless people, and a lot of them are addicts. So he's giving back, and I think that's holding him accountable.

"We have a good relationship with him again. He has a nice young girlfriend. We're thrilled with how he has responded. I still have a little tiny part of me that wonders when the other shoe's going to drop. But I continue to gain more hope and trust as time goes by, as we continue the class and as he continues to do well."

These HopeDealers got their inside world right through Finding Hope, and it's changed the way they see God in the outside world entirely.

Carole's Story

"Samantha was about 14 or 15 years old, and her grades had been falling. She was a freshman in high school, and the first semester of that year, she got straight As. Then the second semester, all of a sudden, she started failing math and not doing well in some other classes. That was our first clue. She had had a falling out with some of her friends and was in transition as far as friendships, and she had picked up a new friend that had a reputation. We monitored where she went and whether she was supervised and so forth, but we had our suspicions about the group of friends she had started hanging out with.

"We found something we thought was pot in her backpack. I had never seen it before, so I wasn't sure if it was or wasn't, and Jeff was kind of the same way, but we quickly, with the help of the internet, figured out it was pot. We brought her upstairs and tried to talk with her about it. We asked her where she got it and whether she had used it and how she was feeling, and she was very honest with us about being very depressed. At that point in time, we talked to her about her depression. We asked her the tough questions, whether she had ever considered taking her own life, and she said, 'Yes.'"

So began Carole's (and her husband Jeff's) travails with

their daughter Samantha. Samantha struggled greatly with depression, so she coped with that through drugs and self-harm. She rebelled against her parental authority for quite some time until Jeff and Carole, exasperated and with no other means of loving their daughter, sent her to Teen Challenge.

Samantha thrived in the yearlong Teen Challenge program, though it was agonizing for Carole to send her daughter off, away from home, for that long. She knew Samantha was safe, but it's still difficult to leave part of your heart that far away, especially knowing all the struggles she would endure through detox and therapy. Samantha made it through, graduated the program, and managed to stay sober for awhile… before falling right back into drug use.

"During that time, I happened to meet a few other mothers whose sons had been in the Teen Challenge program in a different area of Missouri, and they all got on a Sunday night telephone call, where they just talked with one another and shared. I had never experienced anything like it, because when Jeff and I were going through this, we knew nobody else who had these types of issues. We were by ourselves, we were completely isolated in this issue, and so now all of a sudden, I've met these other moms who have sons in the Teen Challenge program, and they helped me with some books and blogs to read, and one of the blogs suggested was Lance Lang's."

And that started Carole's association with Hope Is Alive. Carole began to learn how to see God in the outside world by getting her inside world put right. But, before we can go any further, we have to interrupt Carole's story and talk about the next, all-important chapter of Hope Is Alive.

#NINE

"GO SAVE SOME LIVES"

"You're blessed when you can show people how to cooperate instead of compete or fight. That's when you discover who you really are, and your place in God's family." (Matthew 5:9, MSG)

And now, to tell the story properly, I need to step aside and reintroduce you to my wife, Allyson (whom everyone, including me, calls Ally). Ally and I have been on an interesting ride as I've gone through addiction, recovery, sobriety, and all the steps of Hope Is Alive I've been detailing so far. You may have noticed that, throughout this book, I've been saying "we" a lot instead of "I". That's because Ally has been present for a lot of these steps, though she hasn't always been in the foreground. Ally's story is an *amazing* HopeDealer story, and I'm not just saying that because I'm married to her! I think she has a whole book's worth of story in her, but for now, let's just hit the high points.

I've known Ally for years. I knew her when I was an addict, and we've been through all of the worst of my mess together. But while Ally has largely stuck by me (though she had her own ups and downs), she never really thought she was going to be an integral part of what I was doing with Hope Is Alive.

During much of the time we've covered in this book, Ally started and built a thriving and successful event planning business. Yes, she was with me when I was fired from the treatment center, through the genesis of what would become Hope Is Alive, the tour of the first Hope HQ, and she was incredibly vital for the Nights of Hope; she was always a background presence. Hope Is Alive was my thing and her business was her thing. She never thought she would have a place at HIA other than helping me plan and execute the big things. In the meantime, she had an awesome life that she was chasing after—and succeeding.

But once we started officially dating, Ally would often take her Sunday mornings and come with me to whichever church I happened to be booked in that day. She would support me as I preached and then provide a listening ear afterward when parents inevitably approached me about their addicted child. And she would hear about all these great things we were doing for men, then wonder why we couldn't do something similar for women. But, in her words, by Sunday afternoon, "those thoughts were gone." She had to get back into event-planning mode for the start of the work week.

You have to understand, because of the nature of the event planning business, Ally's life was highly scheduled. She had events lined up that she had to preside over, and so her responsibilities extended a year ahead of her. She had a long-term view, and that view was primarily filled with her business.

But then, on August 31, 2015, Ally sat down at her computer for her daily devotion. Yes, she reads her devotions and then journals at her computer! And in her words, "It was crazy. It was a God moment." She opened a new document and, over what seemed like a timeless moment, typed up an intense and specific plan for a Women's Program at Hope Is Alive.

This was no mere outline—this was a detailed program that included all the usual stuff: the day-to-day schedule, places where we could draw our residents from, curriculum thoughts, and, most surprisingly, Ally's role in all this.

Yes. In that time span, Ally had typed up a completely new career for herself.

And then she slammed the computer shut.

Her words: "I thought, 'Heck no!' I had all this stuff I was already responsible for! I'm so unqualified for this! I'm not a recovering substance abuse addict, I'm a business owner. How could I lead a brand-new program with women who are coming off meth and heroin when I don't even know what that feels like?"

For the next three days, she kept the computer closed and her mouth shut but, thank God, she kept her heart open. She knew she needed to send this plan to me, but she was hesitant. Not just because of the immense life-change it would mean for her, but also because of her lack of experience in full-time ministry. She was waiting for a sign, and she got it when she received a Facebook message that encouraged her to step into her calling, sent from someone who had no idea any of this was percolating.

Ally decided to send the plan to me in an email. Here is a part of what she wrote:

> *My love,*
>
> *I've been praying very hard and working even harder at listening to God's response regarding the HIA Women's Program. With every prayer I lift up, I find myself knowing without a doubt that God has been preparing me for this but even more importantly, our relationship for this.*
>
> *I've innately known since I was a little girl that God gave me a generous heart. With this immense blessing I've had a stirring to give to others beyond measure, to be of service to others in order to fulfill my calling from God. I've had unease about my calling for years, my chosen path seemed like God was making it hard for me. Bringing me frustration, depression, questioning and even at times unfaithfulness to Him. God opened my eyes to understand each and every one of these unwanted attributes were delivered by Him to keep me pushing and searching for a calling He perfectly created me to fulfill.*
>
> *As I write this I can't help but know in God's beauty, He has had a plan for us all along and for the first time I am in a position to see it. I met you before addiction fully grasped you, I lived with you every day during your most active addiction, I was there when HIA was a speck of a dream and I've seen what God has turned it into. Being present*

gives me tremendous insight into the importance of the work of HIA but firsthand experience in the damage, destruction, and desperation addiction causes both for the addict and those surrounding the addict. Going to The Bridge furthered my knowledge in what leads each of us to use for the first time, whether it be drugs, alcohol, food, relationships or any other process addiction. All are a relief from the thoughts swirling in our heads that we are worthless, incapable, unloved, underserving and shunned. I understand each of those feelings, I've done the work to accept why they are there and firmly believe I have the ability to come alongside the recovering and show them the attributes God specifically gave to them.

I want to be your partner in every sense of the word. I want to be a powerhouse couple for God and a tangible example of His mercy everyday. I feel this is where God is calling our relationship and me.

With that being said, I want you to know first and foremost, I understand you are the boss. All decisions lay in your hands for final approval without question. I will give you the respect you so justly deserve. I also realize that all the staff is working toward a single goal and in order to best attain that goal all voices and input are valuable, important and necessary.

Only God has given me the courage and insight to put this down on paper. I realize that I don't have any say in what my role will be but after lots of dedicated prayer and thought *this is where my heart is.*

She sent that to me around midnight and I read it immediately. We already had a lunch date scheduled for the following day, a break in both our busy schedules to spend some time together, and when we met up it was like lightning striking. She was worried I was going to tell her it was a great idea for down the road, but instead I told her what I believed: this was perfect for Hope Is Alive, and she was the one to make it happen.

Because, believe me: when something needs to happen, Ally is the one you want behind the wheel.

"My life changed over the course of that hourlong lunch," Ally likes to say. And while that's true in principle, it didn't change right away. Remember, she had a year of business already booked! If this was going to happen, God was going to have to show up in a huge way.

And you know what? He did.

She had a friend who was also an event planner who'd taken a leave of absence to have a baby but who was getting ready to start everything back up. Ally called her and this woman was able to take over all of Ally's clients. Literally, a year's worth of work, handed over in a 30-minute phone call.

She had to find a house, and that was more difficult. Over the next six weeks she looked at 32 houses, all the time questioning God and feeling discouraged. Sometimes HopeDealers feel discouraged! That's okay! But on Halloween, she went to look at one more house. The owner had given her the code to get in so she could look at it on her own, and from the moment she went in, she knew it was the right place. So she texted the landlord that we were interested and wanted to talk about it. He mentioned that they had a standard contract that he wanted to email her, so she gave him her Hope Is Alive email address and crossed her fingers.

He texted back: *Do you know Lance Lang?*

Now she wondered whether this guy knew me from my drug-related past and whether I owed him money or something. Playing it safe, she texted: *I do. Do you?*

His reply: *Yes. I gave him his first lease on his first house and if you want this for the same reason, it's yours. Go save some lives.*

But it doesn't stop there! God still had more ways to show up for us and for Ally.

Ally set a fundraising goal for $50,000 to launch the program, and to help us reach that goal, we started hosting fundraising dinners in people's homes. We set up five of these home fundraisers, and the first two went pretty well, but they weren't going to smash records or get us anywhere close to the goal we'd set.

Ally went to the third home fundraiser and it started much like the other two had. Worry began to set in as Ally noticed one woman in particular who didn't seem all that enthused about the program. She wouldn't make eye contact and barely maintained any interest. Totally closed down. And as soon as she had the opportunity, the woman took off. It honestly looked to Ally like the woman felt trapped and was looking for a reason to leave.

But she did leave something behind: a check for $50,000.

We lost it. Not the check! I mean that we lost our composure. Ally especially. She had felt so unqualified, and now she had monetary proof that someone believed in her and in the mission she'd typed up on her computer that fateful night. She was absolutely floored that someone would trust her and her vision with that much money, and it completely changed her mindset. She went from "I'm unqualified" to "God is fulfilling our needs at every turn."

Ally is a HopeDealer. She heard God and she knew it would be tough but she said YES. And Hope Is Alive's women's program is going strong as a result.

Stephanie's Story

"Growing up with my dad on staff at a church, as a pastor's kid, was tough. People in town knew me, so my dad would know what I was doing before I got home to tell him. The deacons would call my dad: 'We saw Stephanie on Front Street.' So as soon as I hit the door, it was, 'What were you doing on Front Street?' It was like living in a bubble. Everyone always knew what was going on, sometimes before I even knew it.

"It felt like pressure. Like I was never good enough. Nothing I could do was going to be good enough. I was just always waiting to screw up, because it felt like what everyone was waiting for. I felt like an outsider."

So begins Stephanie's story, with a childhood of unwanted transparency that led to a life of secrecy and disguise.

"I was actually a pretty good kid up until my 10th grade year. My parents moved me to Duncan, Oklahoma from a small town in Mississippi. I hated it. I was mad. I actually remember telling them I was just going to be a pothead and stay in my room. That's not really what happened, but I started hanging out with the wrong crowd.

"I've always made friends pretty easily, and I've always been a chameleon. I can blend in with whomever I need to blend in with. What that looked like is, I started hanging out with older kids who would party, and I started drinking a little bit, and then sneaking off at lunchtime at school to smoke weed in the car, or taking pills while I was at school. I wasn't trashing my life at that point, but I was definitely skewing toward the wrong side of things. I liked being able to fit in."

Stephanie got married right out of high school, and the couple soon had an infant daughter, a responsibility neither of them felt mature enough to handle. Their marriage ended in divorce two months later and Stephanie and her daughter moved in with her parents while trying to set her life back on track. It looked like things were headed that way about a year later when she met and started dating a worship leader for a nearby church.

"We dated for about six months and we got engaged. I thought the heavens had opened and God had given me this really good Christian guy who loved Jesus, who was going to take care of me and take care of my daughter. We got married not too long after that.

"But things changed. I started to see that who he was at church wasn't who he was at home. He started off just being verbally abusive. Then it changed to physically abusive. I lived like that with him for about eight years, which made my drug abuse spiral out of control. I would use more and he would get more mad. I would push his buttons and he would get more mad. It just got worse and worse and worse.

"I was always afraid. If I didn't have all the laundry done by 5:00 when he gets home from work, then, it was over. I was in trouble. It was like, 'You better have this done, or just don't say anything about that, and you'd better sing in the choir on Sunday because that's what you're supposed to do.' It felt like fear but also shame.

"I was two totally different people. I was one person when I was at church and then another person when I was at home. It honestly felt like it did when I was growing up. Those two periods of my life are very similar. It just depended on who I was around. I was a chameleon again."

Stephanie's chameleonic nature allowed her to endure a lot

of pain, but it also led to a horrific internal existence that only got worse when she got pregnant again. Diagnosed early in adulthood with rheumatoid arthritis, Stephanie had been prescribed a mild medication to manage that pain, but the pregnancy meant she had to switch to a medication that wouldn't harm her baby. It wasn't as effective and so once her son was born, her arthritis flared up and her doctors put her on something a little stronger.

"They gave me Oxycontin extended release, and then Oxycontin immediate release. And then my doctor was giving me Percocet for breakthrough pain, so I was super-medicated. I was taking stuff to help me sleep at night. I had bad anxiety so I was taking benzos. I was a train wreck. *And* I had a newborn. *And* I was in an abusive relationship. It was just like, 'Give me more, give me more. I don't care if you hurt me if I can just take something to make me feel better.' So that's just how I lived. I'll just do something to make myself feel better. For six years.

"The first time I OD'd, it was not intentional. I had just taken a lot of Oxy; took a bad cocktail of stuff. I was sitting on my bed, passed out. My parents found me. I wasn't breathing. They called the ambulance. I don't remember anything about the ambulance other than the lights. I woke up three days later, in ICU, on a ventilator. I don't remember the ventilator part, but I remember them pulling that tube out of my throat, and my mom was sitting at the end of my bed. It was the day before Thanksgiving, and she was mad. I didn't know what to say.

"My mom was mad because they didn't understand. They just didn't understand. I remember her saying, 'You almost ruined Thanksgiving.' I know she didn't mean it, like, 'We don't care about what happened to you and you almost ruined our Thanksgiving,' but they didn't know what to do with me anymore. It was just ongoing. I think that hurt was coming out as anger. And I think she was mad because she knew I wasn't ready to be sober. She knew that. She knew what I was going to do when I left the hospital.

"The second time I OD'd, I was in the bathroom at my parents' house. They heard a noise and didn't know what it was. They came in and I had fallen over into the bathtub. My dad was shaking me, trying to get me to come to life. He said I was white as a ghost. I know he hit me in the face pretty hard, just trying to get me to come back, not trying to be mean. He thought I was dying.

"I remember them moving me to the hallway, to where I was laying in the hallway floor. I don't remember a lot, but I remember my daughter getting up out of her bed, stepping over me, and going to my parents' bed. So it wasn't even a new thing for her, like, 'Mom's passed out, dying on the floor.' Most kids would be like, 'Oh my gosh, what's happening?' But it was just normal.

"I remember laying there and my dad saying, 'You need help!' And then I was in the hospital again. And that's right before I got sober. That was the last time that ever happened. That was definitely the lowest. And I was super-mad at my dad for saying that to me. I was mad that he told me I needed help, because I felt like I was at my lowest. I didn't need a self-righteous person telling me that. I think it hurt the most because I knew it was true, but I'd been fighting this for so long. And I was scared."

Stephanie's brain finally got the message that the rest of her body had been sending for years: that she couldn't continue living this way. She went to treatment and began to seek her true identity in Christ. She needed to stop being a chameleon and start being Stephanie.

Stephanie is a helper and she began to feel a burden to help women who were in recovery like her. I had spoken before at her dad's church in Duncan and had even done a roundtable discussion with some of the staff there (including, before I knew who she was, Stephanie) about recovery in the church. And so knowing who I was and what I did, Stephanie reached out to me with an email, telling me that if we ever did something for women that she'd like to help with it.

Here's the fun part about that: I got that message the day before we announced our women's program. Literally hours before. We'd been planning this thing, laying the groundwork for weeks, and Stephanie had no idea! Needless to say, I wrote her back and it wasn't long before Stephanie was at our women's home.

"Hope Is Alive has given me freedom. I might've come here sober, but I wasn't whole. There's a big difference. Understanding how much God accepts me has played a huge role in my recovery, because it's taken off the chains from the past. I know it's there, but I don't have to stay there. God accepts it. God accepts me.

So it's helped me to give other people acceptance. When I know I'm accepted, it helps me accept other people. And accepting other people is what has helped me stay sober.

"I definitely grew up hearing that, if I didn't do my chores right, as unto the Lord, then I wasn't pleasing Him. So I would fold my t-shirts a couple of times to make sure they were right, because that's how Jesus would want my t-shirts folded. And that's not realistic at all. I don't know if Jesus really cares about how my t-shirts are folded; I do know that He cares about what's in my heart. But I had that kind of a mindset, probably until a couple of years ago."

Stephanie became a leader almost immediately, and she hasn't stopped. In fact, not only is she helping to lead our women's program, but Stephanie now also works full-time in our offices, always challenging herself and the rest of us to keep moving forward.

"Since being at Hope Is Alive, it's fostered my relationship with Christ and with other people. I've learned more of what it's like to not be selfish. My relationship with God has grown exponentially. It's the best it's ever been. I'm steadily being pushed to be better, and I've learned that I can always be better. And I like it. It's good. It feels good to grow."

Carole's Story, Continued

Back to the story I started in the previous chapter. Carole's daughter Samantha had gone through Teen Challenge twice, but wasn't finding long-lasting sobriety, and Carole was at a loss. Until a friend of hers connected her with my website and Carole came across a blog post of mine called "What Happens After Rock Bottom." Of course, I talked a lot about the benefits of sober living in that post, because I talk a lot about it all the time. It was the first time Carole had ever heard the term.

"It made total sense," she says. "When we were going through all the issues after Teen Challenge, we knew something had been missing; we knew there was some kind of transition piece between such a controlled environment to living life normally that we missed. And that was sober living."

Carole called the phone number that I had listed in the blog post and I happened to be the one to answer it that day. I was so glad to be able to tell her that we were starting a women's program later that month. I counseled her for a bit, gave her some thoughts and options, and left it open-ended for her, her husband Jeff, and Samantha to talk things over.

"Lance gave me Allyson's phone number. I wrote Allyson's name and phone number on a little note card, and Samantha took that note card and threw it at me in her room, like, 'There's no way I'm looking at doing something like this.' I went about the rest of my day, and later on I got a text from her: 'Mom, I called Allyson and talked to her, and it sounds like something I want to do.'

"When I had called Lance on the phone and talked to him

about the sober living home, he told me there's two things. One, if you can get her down here to see the home; she's going to love the home, it's beautiful. And the second thing, when she gets here, she's going to realize that sober living can be fun, and those two things will make a difference in her life. And Lance was spot-on with those two things.

"We drove to the home Saturday after Thanksgiving in the middle of an ice storm, just to get her there, and the house really was beautiful. The house manager and assistant house manager and Allyson were all there, and they couldn't have been more welcoming to Samantha. It was like she had instant friends.

"For me, it was comforting, because I knew these friends would be a positive influence on her. These were adult women who could help her transition from being a teenager to being an adult and living an adult life in a sober manner. It was wonderful. It was God-ordained, I am absolutely, 100% sure, because she moved in the week before the opening of that home, and she's been there ever since, and I don't think a day goes by where she doesn't say she loves life.

"It just makes our hearts so happy to see her back to being the type of child that she was, where she's happy and she's fearless and she's full of life and vigor. She's anxious to learn about the Lord and she's anxious to study in college again and to build a future for herself where she can do something to help other people learn what she's learned."

Samantha is now a HopeDealer, and we couldn't be happier.

#TEN

HATERS GONNA HATE

"You're blessed when your commitment to God provokes persecution. The persecution drives you even deeper into God's kingdom." (Matthew 5:10, MSG)

One thing I didn't expect when I started Hope Is Alive was the hate. I guess it's because I wasn't paying attention to those parts of the Bible, because the Bible talks about this a lot. We even see this in this chapter's Beatitude.

When you decide to tell your story, some people are going to come at you. And the more you tell it, the more you get your story out there, the more people will decide they don't like what you're doing and will speak out against you, either to your face or to your circle of friends or supporters.

And you know what? *That's okay.*

It doesn't have to affect you.

Some people just don't understand the importance of

vulnerability. It makes them uncomfortable. Or maybe they know they should be telling their story but they don't want to, so they feel convicted. Or maybe they're dealing with some hurt or pain or addiction in their own lives and they don't like the reminder that your story brings. They aren't ready to deal with it yet, so they try to drown out the noise by bringing you down. Or maybe they don't get why you're doing what you're doing, so they lash out. There can be all kinds of reasons why people bring in negativity, but those reasons are theirs, not yours.

When you decide to become a HopeDealer, negativity will come. Just accept it and keep dealing. Because ultimately people hate on what they don't understand. And a HopeDealer, devoted to sharing the pain of their past for the sole reason of helping others, can be hard to understand.

People have tried to hate on me and Hope Is Alive, and when they do, I do my best not to take it personally. They aren't hating *me*; they're hating the Christ *in* me. I'm reminded not only of this particular Beatitude that we used to start this chapter, but also of the following few verses that Jesus uses to tie a bow on the Beatitudes. Here they are:

"Not only that—count yourselves blessed every time people put you down or throw you out or speak lies about you to discredit me. What it means is that the truth is too close for comfort and they are uncomfortable. You can be glad when that happens— give a cheer, even!—for though they don't like it, *I* do! And all heaven applauds. And know that you are in good company.

My prophets and witnesses have always gotten into this kind of trouble." (Matthew 5:11-12, MSG)

The truth of the matter is, it's not the HopeDealer's job to make everyone understand or even to get everyone to like them. That's an addict's mindset. Addicts are people-pleasers. We want everyone to like us, but that's only because addicts don't understand unconditional love in relationships. All our relationships are transactional—if I can get people to like me, then they might give me drugs or money to buy drugs. It's all about what you can get from a person.

The HopeDealer doesn't think like this. The HopeDealer doesn't worry about pleasing everyone. In fact, I'd go so far as to say the HopeDealer doesn't worry about pleasing *anyone but God*. That's the way you as a HopeDealer stay on mission, stay true to the story that God has written with your life, the song that He gave you to sing after He lifted you out of that pit and set your feet on solid ground. You do what you're supposed to do and be solid to your foundation in Christ.

This doesn't make sense to the outsider. To the unbeliever, it's perfectly acceptable to hit back at your haters, but that is not the Christian way. And I mean that word *Christian* in its literal sense: *Christ-like*.

If we HopeDealers are serious about being Christ-like, then we must emulate Christ, a Man who knew He was going to be betrayed by one of His closest friends and still told that friend to do it. A Man who was convicted of a crime He didn't commit and who, when He had the opportunity to defend Himself in court, said, "It is as you say." He let them hate when He knew all He had done was love.

That's the difficulty of living as a HopeDealer. But once you've started to deal hope, there's no other way to live that makes as much sense. In fact, when I hear grumbling or gossip I try to do what the verse says, and be glad! I cheer about it. I think about Heaven rejoicing over the fact that my willingness to be vulnerable has caused others so much discomfort they've chosen to hate. That's crazy to think about, and it's counterintuitive to our sensitive human nature, but it's the best way to live. So slap on the blinders, set out to tell your story, and just stay focused on the path in front of you. Haters gonna hate but we've got no time to waste on that; there are too many people needing what only we have!

Sow Your Seed

If you've been in church for any amount of time (especially a Baptist church, where evangelism is so emphasized), you've probably heard Jesus' Parable of the Sower:

"Listen! A farmer went out to plant some seed. As he scattered it across his field, some of the seed fell on a footpath, and the birds came and ate it. Other seed fell on shallow soil with underlying rock. The seed sprouted quickly because the soil was shallow. But the plant soon wilted under the hot sun, and since it didn't have deep roots, it died. Other seed fell among thorns that grew up and choked out the tender plants so they produced no grain. Still other seeds fell on fertile soil, and they sprouted, grew, and produced a crop that was thirty, sixty, and even a hundred times as much as had been planted! ...Anyone with ears to hear should listen and understand." (Mark 4:3-9, NLT)

Now, all my life I've heard this parable and thought it was about making sure that you plant seeds in good soil, that the fertile soil is the place where you'll get the harvest. And that's very true!

But the more I think about it, the more I noticed something: *the sower sows everywhere.* The sower isn't worried about the kind of ground they're sowing on! The sower isn't worried they're going to run out of seed or that they're wasting their time sowing in all these crazy places where they can never expect to receive a harvest! What's the sower doing throwing seed down on a footpath anyway?

It's crazy when you start to think about it, until you realize that the sower's job is not to create a harvest—the sower's job is just to sow.

This is the job of the HopeDealer. You are not responsible for a harvest; you're only responsible for sowing your seed—telling your story—and letting God take care of the harvest part. When people finally have their ears ready, they'll be able to hear you.

If you'll recall, Blake came to a Night of Hope. He wasn't ready yet to go into recovery, but he said the event put a seed in his brain. I'm picturing one of those seeds that fell on the footpath that got eaten by a bird. You know what happens to seeds when they get eaten by birds? Nothing! Yet. They might get digested by that bird, but seeds are tough, and often they will make it through the bird's digestive system and come out the other end. And you know birds like to hang out in trees, so that seed may wind up falling out of that tree and into some good ground!

You never know the journeys your seeds of hope might take; that's why Jesus tells you to sow them without worry. You aren't going to run out of hope anymore than that sower in Jesus' parable was going to run out of seed. In fact, I've found that, the more I sow seeds of hope as a HopeDealer, the more hope I have to deal.

And that's the future of Hope Is Alive: sowing seeds on all kinds of ground. We want to tell our story, and we want to add your voice, if you're willing. Hope Is Alive is just a bunch of HopeDealers, people who have seen rock bottom, who have been lifted out of a pit, and who have been set on solid ground and who now want to sing our songs to an audience filled with people who need to hear them, whether they realize that yet or not. And really, to an Audience of One.

#ELEVEN

THE ULTIMATE GOAL

At the beginning of this book, I briefly mentioned the story found in Joshua 3:7-4:24, about the Israelites crossing the Jordan river and into the Promised Land. The story is too long to reproduce in these pages, but here's the gist:

The Israelites had spent 40 years wandering in the desert, waiting to be able to go into the Promised Land. And now the time had arrived! Their story of aimlessness and purposelessness was about to change and they were finally about to embrace their destiny. But they had to cross the Jordan River first, and this was no piddly stream. This was an actual, for-real river. They didn't know a thing about orbit or satellites at the time, but this river is the kind you can see from space (if you squint just right).

There wasn't a bridge to cross or a handy barge that could handle 40,000 Israelites, so it was up to God to provide a miracle. Echoing the miracle that He provided when He'd led the Israelites out of Egypt all those years before, He stopped the waters of the Jordan from flowing so that they could cross it on dry land.

And that's just what they did. The entire nation of Israelites walked across the Jordan and made it safely to the other side. But Joshua, their leader, told some men to grab some stones from the bottom of the river. And then those men carried those stones from the bottom of the river and up into the Promised Land. They carried those stones all the way into the land until the Israelites set up camp, and then they stacked those stones and made them a monument.

Why? Joshua tells us:

"When your children ask their parents in time to come, 'What do these stones mean?' then you shall let your children know, 'Israel crossed over the Jordan here on dry ground.' For the Lord your God dried up the waters of the Jordan for you until you crossed over, as the Lord your God did to the Red Sea, which he dried up for us until we crossed over, so that all the peoples of the earth may know that the hand of the Lord is mighty, and so that you may fear the Lord your God forever." (Joshua 4:21b-24, NRSV)

Those stones came from the *literal rock bottom* to become a storytelling prompt for generations to come. Joshua had them taken and set up in a place where everyone could see them so that everyone who encountered them would know what God had done for the Israelites.

The stones became the story.

That's what HopeDealers do.

HopeDealers are just people who are willing to say YES.

YES to their story.

YES to others.

YES to sharing.

YES to sowing the seeds of hope.

Sometimes it seems counterintuitive. Sometimes it can be painful. But we HopeDealers must do it.

I have one more story to tell you.

Zach A.'s Story

I recently had the heart-rending privilege of preaching at the funeral for one of our guys. Zach Arismendez was a HopeDealer who died clean and sober from a surprise heart attack at the age of 32. I'll never forget him.

There's a photo of Zach that will be permanently etched in my memory. It's of him, hugging his mother at the front of a church, holding a sign that had one simple word on it, written in Zach's handwriting:

Forgiven.

This was August 12 of 2016, just two months after he'd joined up with Hope Is Alive.

Zach knew not only that God had forgiven him, but even

more importantly… Zach had also forgiven himself.

"I was hopeless, I had tons of shame," Zach had written around that time. "Most of my shame was over how I treated my family and the things I did to them. I had betrayed my family over and over again for years and I didn't think that I could ever get their trust back.

"It wasn't until I quit worrying about being forgiven and started utilizing the tools of the Hope is Alive program that I was able to be forgiven. Things didn't start to change for me and my family until I completely gave things to God. I had to stop trying to fix things on my own and ask for help."

The photo of Zach and his mother gives me such hope. I look at it and I see a snapshot of so many of our HopeDealers' stories. Because a new life of freedom awaits us all, at the moment we forgive ourselves, and Zach taught us all so much about forgiveness.

Many years, of course, had led up to this picture. And these years are what makes this image so powerful. Zach had struggled feeling comfortable in his own skin from early on. Growing up he had always been taller than his classmates. Combine that with what could be a shy (to say the least) personality and that made for some awkward years that only got worse as Zach slid into addiction. But as he began to get clean, he found hope. And he also began to find comfort in his own skin.

About two months before this photo, Zach's sweet mother Dawn, who was always trying to help him be the best any way she could, was handed a brochure about Hope is Alive. From there she made Zach do exactly what she should have: she made him call, seek out the help for himself, and I believe that is one of the main reasons why everyone in our ministry got the incredible privilege of spending his last year with him clean and sober.

Zach soon found recovery, yes, but he wasn't the only one affected. His parents, Mike and Dawn, also embraced recovery for themselves. I have never seen a family so willing to do whatever it takes to find help. They sought out a new life because of how much they loved each other and how much they loved their son. As HopeDealers, they taught me and so many others what it looks like to love unconditionally. To go to any lengths to learn, grow, and become the best versions of themselves that they could. Zach had great parents and he loved them so much.

But in addition to the photo I've talked about, there's a passage in the Bible that will forever remind me of Zach. It was his favorite verse and it is this:

"Therefore, since we are surrounded by such a great cloud of witnesses, let us throw off everything that hinders and the sin that so easily entangles. And let us run with perseverance the race marked out for us, fixing our eyes on Jesus, the pioneer and perfecter of faith." (Hebrews 12:1-2, NIV)

Zach spent the last year of his life surrounded by such a great cloud of witnesses. He wasn't holed up somewhere he shouldn't be. He wasn't sitting in shame, he wasn't paralyzed by fear, he wasn't out hurting people or hurting himself.

No, he was surrounded by people who loved him.

And not only was he surrounded, but he'd also thrown off all the sin, muck, and mire that had entangled him for so many years. He had worked through his past, he had accepted Jesus as the Lord of his life, and he was living that life out.

Because of this new commitment in his life, Zach was living out the gifts that come with a life devoted to God:

"But what happens when we live God's way? He brings gifts into our lives, much the same way that fruit appears in an orchard—things like affection for others, exuberance about life, serenity. We develop a willingness to stick with things, a sense of compassion in the heart, and a conviction that a basic holiness permeates things and people. We find ourselves involved in loyal commitments, not needing to force our way in life, able to marshal and direct our energies wisely." (Galatians 5:22-23, MSG)

That describes Zach to a T. He was a quiet encourager. He was so thoughtful, he always spoke carefully and deliberately, he was never critical, never judgmental, and he stood up for what he believed in and Who he believed in.

Zach was a special kind of HopeDealer, the kind who can draw you in, make you love them, push you to root for them and cheer them on, and yet never say a word.

Zach was a leader, but not someone who had to lead from the front. Instead, he led from the middle of the pack, and that takes rare and unique leadership. He didn't have to be out front, he didn't need to be the loudest voice. Because he knew his voice, he knew who he was, because he knew *Whose* he was.

He was humble, he was willing, he was self-less.

He was a HopeDealer.

The week between Zach's death and his funeral, I heard so many stories about Zach that I'd never heard before. Like how, after working late into the night, Zach would drive across town to pick up a guy in our program who needed a ride so he could be at work at 3:30 in the morning.

When his new roommate moved in and he was too big for the bed he was assigned, Zach said, "Here, you can have my bed."

When Zach was asked to do anything, his answer was always YES!

Zach was forgiven, he was surrounded by family, he possessed the fruits of the Spirit, he knew his purpose, he ran his race…

Zach left us clean, sober, and saved.

And he was a HopeDealer to the very end.

Zach's legacy is one of hope, one that proves that people really do change. A legacy that shows that love casts out all fear. A legacy that shows the impact you can make by just listening to someone as they share.

A legacy that will always remind us that hope is alive!

That's the goal of every HopeDealer, to pass from this earth having left a legacy. Having made a positive impact, even if it was just on one person.

We all have the potential to become HopeDealers because we've all experienced some type of pain and heartache. There's no one immune to disaster or tragedy. We are all lumped into that category. What sets a HopeDealer apart is the willingness to take the pain and use it for good. It's the desire to turn a negative into a positive. To use what the enemy meant for evil and turn to something good.

As you've read throughout this book, God loves to tell a comeback story. God is still working miracles today. You are one of them! Don't sit on the special work that God has done to bring you to this place of restoration. Choose to pass it along to the hundreds, the thousands, the millions who need what you have.

You have a special kind of hope. It's *your* hope. It's unique to *you*. And if you have trouble believing you're that special, I don't know what to tell you other than this: *you are*. You don't need a testimony that starts with you lying on a dirty air mattress surrounded by used heroin needles. You don't need to have OD'd or died. You don't need to have married an alcoholic or sunk half your family's finances into treatment after treatment after treatment. You don't need a master's in divinity from a prestigious school. You don't need a pulpit in front of a church of thousands.

All you need is a story. Your story.

Today is the day you start to tell your HopeDealer story. Don't waste another moment. Sow the seeds. Sing your song.

Deal some hope.

Because hope is alive.

A WORD AFTER

TAKE ACTION

Thanks for taking the time to read this book! I hope it captivated you, motivated you, and prepared you to go tell your HopeDealer story! My hope is that you will choose to join the HopeDealer movement and help us spread hope across the world!

Remember: your story is so powerful! It's unique, yet perfectly suited to help someone else who is going through what you've overcome.

So today I want to encourage you to join us in this moment and post your story on our new HopeDealers website. By doing so, people from all over the world will have the opportunity to hear about what you've been through and how God has rescued you, put your feet on a firm foundation, and given you a story to tell.

Your story is your secret weapon of hope, and we want to give you a way to target that weapon so you can hit the world with it.

The process is simple:

1. Visit www.HopeDealers.com

2. Record or Write your #HopeDealer story

3. Submit it

4. We will review it and post it

To show our appreciation for your willingness to be a HopeDealer, we will send you a free t-shirt! When you wear it, you'll be sure to catch some attention, and when you do, be ready to share your story and point them to the website to view your story and the story of other HopeDealers!

Together we can change the world! One story at a time!

ONE MORE THING!

As we prepared to write this new book, we sat down for formal interviews with many of the HopeDealers we profiled here. And guess what: we filmed them. If you want to hear more about their stories, visit our new HopeDealers website to watch all the films.

www.HopeDealers.com.

ABOUT LANCE LANG

Lance has devoted his life to inspiring hope in all those he comes across. His powerful story of overcoming addiction has touched the lives of thousands of people across the country. Lance is the leader & founder of Hope is Alive Ministries. An organization whose mission is to, *radically change the lives of drug addicts, alcoholics & those that love them.*

Lance is successful blogger and a sought-after speaker who is known for his ability to speak directly to the heart of any audience. Lance shares his story weekly at churches, prisons, schools, treatment facilities and men's groups.

Connect with Lance:

@LanceLang   Lance@LanceLang.com

ALSO AVAILABLE FROM LANCE:

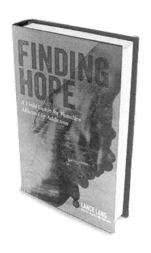

Worry. Fear. Pain. You think something might be wrong with your loved one—your son or daughter, your husband or wife, your mom or dad—but you can't be sure. Can it just be a phase they're going through, or can it be something worse? Can it even be addiction?

Finding Hope was written with you in mind. Starting from diagnosing whether your loved one has a problem with addiction, and taking you all the way through treatment and beyond, Lance Lang has created this field manual to help both you and your loved one get the help you both need. Packed with useful information, practical steps, and encouraging interviews, Finding Hope is your foundational resource for navigating the traumatic upheaval of addiction.

Dreams are universal. The hopes we all have for our future, the plans we all sketch out in our minds. And then, somewhere along the way, those dreams slip out of our grasp. Whether through some kind of pain or worry, some guilt or mistake, or just the dull routine of life getting in the way, we lose hope and start to slide into normality. But it doesn't have to be this way! Those dreams can fuel your world once more, you just have to discover the transformative power of hope.

This book is the story of how my hope departed, how it was restored, and how I've kept it alive. I wrote it for drug addicts, alcoholics, gamblers, sex addicts, hurt people, prideful people, and angry people. I wrote it for the fear-ridden, the guilty, the insecure, the obsessed, the perpetually disappointed, and anyone else caught in the tornado of destruction that is addiction.

The Hope Handbook is the corresponding guidebook that takes the reader deeper into each chapter, allowing them the opportunity to share about their personal experiences and participate in activities created to solidify the teaching while offering therapeutic times of mediation, music and prayer.

HOPE IS ALIVE

Hope is Alive exists to radically change the lives of drug addicts, alcoholics & those that love them. HIA is at the forefront of the addition recovery community, working hard every day to help people find hope. We work with families, addicts in addiction, addicts in recovery, pastors, church leaders, counseling professionals, interventionists and many more. Here are some of the ways HIA can help you!

HIA Mentoring Homes: For five years now HIA has lead the way in creating transformational sober living environments. Hundreds of men and women have been impacted through our unique and individualized approach. Located in Oklahoma City & Tulsa, the HIA Mentoring Homes are provide individuals who transitioning back into the real world from treatment and correctional facilities a path towards successful long-term sobriety. Over the past five years the HIA Mentoring Homes have enjoyed a 90% success rate for all graduates! Our success is found in our long-term (18 month), customized, intentional program that gives the addict the opportunity to not only establish a strong foundation of sobriety, but a firm footing in all facets of their lives. Residents leave our program equipped emotionally, professionally, spiritually, and financially along with a toolkit of life skills that enable them to contribute mightily to their respective community.

For more information on the HIA Mentoring Homes please visit **www.HopeisAlive.net** or call 1.844.3.HopeNow

Finding Hope Support Groups: Hope is Alive has developed a one of a kind, faith based support group for loved-ones of addicts & alcoholics. Through curriculum developed by Lance & Ally Lang (Founders of Hope is Alive), loved-ones are able find hope through education and a caring community of like-minded individuals. The class is offered free to the public in several cities across Oklahoma. To find a location or to find out how you can start your own Finding Hope group in your community, visit **www.FindingHope.Today**

Church Partnership Program: We consult and partner with churches to provide their staff a "first responder" in times of addiction crisis, while also providing their congregation with valuable resources and referral options.

Family Services: Hope is Alive provides referral services, interventions, family consulting and free resources to individuals across the country. Visit **www.HopeisAlive.net/Resources** to find our list of trusted resources.

To find out more about Hope is Alive Ministries visit us at www.HopeisAlive.net or connect with us socially.

Made in the USA
Columbia, SC
03 January 2020